A TREATISE

ON

HELIOCHROMY;

OR,

The Production of Pictures,

BY MEANS OF LIGHT,

IN NATURAL COLORS.

EMBRACING

A Full, Plain, and Unreserved Description

OF THE PROCESS KNOWN AS

THE HILLOTYPE,

INCLUDING THE AUTHOR'S NEWLY DISCOVERED

COLLODIO-CHROME,

OR NATURAL COLORS ON COLLODIONIZED GLASS.

TOGETHER WITH

Various Processes for Natural Colors,

ON PAPER, VELVET, PARCHMENT, SILK, MUSLIN, PORCELAIN, WOOD, &c.,

AND ELABORATE ESSAYS

ON THE THEORY OF LIGHT AND COLORS, THE CHEMISTRY OF HELIOCHROMY, AND THE ENTIRE RANGE OF THE AUTHOR'S NINE YEARS' EXPERIENCE IN SUN COLORING.

BY L. L. HILL.

OF WESTKILL, GREENE CO., N. Y.

PUBLISHED BY ROBINSON & CASWELL,

57 CHAMBERS STREET, N. Y.

1856.

Printed by R. Craighead,
53 Vesey street.

PREFACE.

A Preface should be brief. It is not in good taste for an author to puff his own book; and prefaces, as generally written, are most egregious laudations of the author's production.

I will not indulge in so unpalatable an imposition on the reader's good sense; but I will be bold enough to say, that this book, with all its imperfections, is about as well got up as could be expected. The theme is original, and of course, I have had very little help from other writers. Alone, almost without chart or compass, I have discovered and explored a new and beautiful art region. For long years I have traversed this bewitching clime, this magic land, this "Beulah" of Photography; and if, after all my exciting revels, I have given a *correct description* of the "beauties of the place," I beg pardon of all the unmerciful critics, when I say that I have a claim on their kind forbearance.

Success and immortal honor to the next adventurer, whoever he may be, who shall go where I have been, and who, perhaps, shall dive into regions beyond, and bring back garlands of exceeding and unfading beauty. Henceforth may the progress of the *Heliochrome* be onward, and may the time be near when it shall crown with an ambrosial diadem every other branch of the Photographic Art.

L. L. HILL.

WESTKILL, GREENE CO., N. Y.,
June 19*th*, 1856.

Contents.

AUTOBIOGRAPHY OF THE AUTHOR.

CHAPTER I.

CHAPTER II.

TREATISE ON HELIOCHROMY.

CHAPTER I.

CHAPTER II.

CHAPTER III.

CHAPTER IV.

CHAPTER V.

CHAPTER VI.

CHEMISTRY OF HELIOCHROMY.

CHAPTER VII.

EXPERIMENTS ON THE DAGUERREOTYPE PLATE.

CHAPTER VIII.

EXPERIMENTS WITH VARIOUS METALS.

CHAPTER IX.

EXPERIMENTS WITH THE SALTS OF THE METALS.

CHAPTER X.

EXPERIMENTS WITH VEGETABLE JUICES.

CHAPTER XI.

NATURAL COLORS ON PAPER.

CHAPTER XII.

HELIOCHROMES ON TEXTILE FABRICS.

CHAPTER XIII.

NATURAL COLORS ON GLASS.

CHAPTER XIV.

THE HILLOTYPE.

CHAPTER XV.

MISCELLANY.

CHAPTER XVI.

DESCRIPTION OF THE PHOTOGRAPHS.

AUTOBIOGRAPHY OF THE AUTHOR.

CHAPTER I.

Place of his Birth—His Parents—Murder of his Father—Apprentice at Printing—McNaughton, the Scotch Artist—Christian Experience, and call to the Ministry—Works for Horace Greeley—Impressions of Greeley—Studies for the Ministry—Becomes Pastor at New Baltimore—Courtship and Marriage—The Mountain Girl—Ministry at Westkill—Antinomianism—Anti-Rent War—Plain Preaching—Becomes Publisher—Removes to Saugerties—Attacked with the Bronchitis—Quits Preaching—Goes to Daguerreotyping—Early Lessons in the Art—The Blues, the Fog, the Blacks—Travelling Daguerreotypist—Good Success—Durand the Artist—Called Home—The Hurricane—Views of Medicine—Begins Experimenting for the Natural Colors—Treatise on Daguerreotype—The Magic Buff—Photographic Researches—Pupils—Pecuniary Affairs.

I WAS born in the village of Athens, Greene Co., New York, February 26, 1816. My father, Lee Lawrence Hill, was a Commissary in the Army of 1812–13, and was brought home wounded by three bullets, two of which he carried in his flesh till he died. In the month of July, 1828, he was murdered by the hands of three young men, as we of the family are well satisfied, for the gratification of a family spite, growing out of some legal difficulties. Thus, at the age of twelve years, I was left under the care of my mother, and few lads were ever as well cared for as I was by her. Wisely, piously, and assiduously, did she fulfil her mission towards a large family of children.

At the age of thirteen years, I was placed an apprentice at printing, in the office of the *Hudson Gazette*, to which city our family had removed previous to my father's death. There, under the kind care of Hiram Wilbur, Esq., I soon became an expert typo, and in his amiable family was, I dare say, as happy as Ben. Franklin in the palmiest days of his minority. After remaining with Mr. Wilbur about two years, I became clerk in a store, but after a few months returned to typography, in the office of the *Rural Repository*. While in the store, I fell acquainted with James McNaughton, Esq., a Scotch artist of no small distinction. From him I learned the first rudiments of drawing and painting—miniature painting, particularly. I remember, distinctly, that on seeing him at work on a miniature of one of my sisters, I felt that I could willingly part with my left hand, if by so doing my right hand could be trained to the beautiful art. Mr. McNaughton afterwards removed to the city of New York, and after the lapse of a few months I followed him thither, with a view of placing myself under his care and tuition. Being a stranger in the great metropolis, I searched for my friend in vain for many days. The most I could learn about him was that he had been very sick with inflammatory rheumatism, and was reduced to great poverty. One day in my rambles in Broadway, I was pushing my inquiries among the artists, and in the studio of a miniature painter my eye rested upon one of McNaughton's off-hand sketches, upon the merits of which the artist and some friends were expatiating in terms of high compliment. From them I learned that the object of my search was in the hospital, sick with the *small-pox*. My dread of this horrible disease was intense; but having been vaccinated, I repaired at once to the hospital. After pressing my suit for some time, I was admitted to his room. He knew me at once, and exclaimed—"Gracious God! my dear boy, what brought you here!" "To see you, and try to comfort you," was my reply. "Bless God," said he,

" out of all my acquaintances this side of the great ocean, I have one friend." He then told me that he was going to die, and directed me where to find a miniature of himself, his easel, his paints, his brushes, all which he gave me as his last legacy. I visited him several times after this, gave him twenty dollars in money (nearly all I had), and when I called the last time, I learned that he was dead and buried. Were it possible to recall our friends from the dead, James McNaughton, the friend of my early days, the man who first developed in my soul a passion for *delineation in color*, would be one of the first I should summon.

Soon after this, our family having removed to the village of Kingston, I entered the office of the *Ulster Plebeian*, where I remained over a year. The family of the amiable editor, John Tappan, Esq., were a second Wilbur family to me, and I shall never forget their old-fashioned Dutch intelligence and kindness. During my stay with Mr. Tappan I occupied most of my leisure hours in study. The method I pursued was somewhat novel, and exceedingly profitable to me. Whatever subjects of interest I put in type through the day, I investigated at night. Thus, my daily toils formed a portion of my studies. For example—did I " set up " an anecdote of Franklin?—I read his life that night; an article on the " Variations of the Compass?"—that night I turned navigator; was the subject Murder—Matrimony—Potatoes—Zoology—Sugar Candy—Mexico—Tecumseh—Conchology—Peaches—Political Economy—Prussian Blue—Sealing-Wax—I swallowed my supper, and made for the Encyclopædia.

To tell the whole truth, I had, at this time, an associate of rather dissipated habits. He was possessed of a most brilliant intellect, and might have been a star in our nation; but he died of the *delirium tremens*. The talents of this young man (who shall be nameless here) were of an extraordinary character. He would frequently, after a hard day's work, write a " Tale " for some Magazine, which would be thankfully accepted, and he would then go to bed drunk, in sight of the morning star, work ten hours next day, and write a poem at night. A poem which he wrote, under the title of "*The Carriers' Address*," was pronounced by good judges, equal to Byron's best. It was composed of some two hundred lines, and I am witness to the fact, that he composed it within the space of four hours, for I put it into type. Twenty years have passed since my acquaintance with this young man, and I shall never cease to regret that, for a short time, I was too much influenced by the bad part of his example.

Soon after these events, I became associated with a circle of young men and women who were in the habit of attending Baptist prayer meetings. I had about this time frequented the Methodist church, where I was much interested, and somewhat impressed, by the preaching of the Rev. Mr. Foss, a minister of fervent piety and peculiar eloquence. Now a powerful revival commenced among my young friends, and I was induced, by their urgent entreaties, to go and see what the Lord was doing. The meetings were held at private houses, and at the very first I attended I felt that God was in the place. My companions, it seemed to me, were of the elect, and the Lord was now separating them unto himself, while I was to be left behind. Conviction for sin rolled upon my mind like a mighty wave, but I could see no hope. Despair—withering, blighting despair—seized my inmost soul, and I felt myself sinking to the deeps of hell. Long years ago I had promised my Maker to seek his face—but I had broken my vows; and now a voice seemed to say: "He is joined to his idols; let him alone." Once, in particular, while I resided in the city of Hudson, I was brought very low, and the Lord heard my cry. It was on the Sabbath day, and, contrary to the express injunction of my mother, I was skating on the frozen river, and was plunged into an air-hole. I suffered all the pangs of drowning, but was rescued; and after two hours' diligent effort, by the hands of strangers, I was restored. While in the water, I felt as any sinner would be likely to feel under similar circumstances. I vowed most earnestly, that if the Lord would deliver me I would serve him all the days of my life. This vow I had broken, and now, after the lapse of years, it weighed heavy upon my soul. For four days and nights I could neither eat nor sleep—pleasure lost its charms and the world its beauty, and wherever I went creation itself seemed frowning and howling upon the reprobate. But the Spirit of God did not leave me; I was sweetly led out of this "iron cage of despair" into a "large place." Young converts and aged saints took me by the hand and led me to Jesus; and I saw the loving Lamb of God by the eye of faith, and he did not frown, but accepted the "weapons of my rebellion," and filled my soul with "peace in believing, and joy in the Holy Spirit." Blessed and adored be his holy name!—that "glad hour" was to me the beginning of "joys that cannot be expressed." It may seem odd to some of my brother daguerreotypists, that I should tell my experience in a book on Heliochromy; but this simple tale will hurt nobody, while the record of it, in this very volume, relieves my own conscience. I am an imperfect man; but God only knows how utterly unendurable my late labors and trials would have been, had I not felt that I had a God to go to.

Having united with the Baptist Church in Kingston, I found myself most pleasantly employed in publishing the glad news of salvation to all I met. In the conference meetings especially, I was at home; and I can truly say that those were the happiest days of my life. A few months after my union with the church, I was licensed to preach the gospel, and I at once repaired to the Literary and Theological Seminary (now Madison University) at Hamilton, Madison Co., N. Y., to study for the work. There I remained between four and five years; and then, with a view of raising funds to support myself in theological studies two years longer, I went to work at my trade in the city of New York, where I remained about one year. The star of Horace Greeley was then rising in brilliancy, and I for a short time immortalized some of his editorials for the "*New Yorker*." My acquaintance with him was not intimate, but I formed a profound estimate of his genius and amiability. I also worked on the "*Courier and Inquirer*," and other morning papers, where I formed the abominable habit of keeping late hours; and to this day, my time for getting sleepy is between 11 o'clock P.M. and 1 o'clock A.M. While at Hamilton I supported myself mainly by my earnings during the vacations. I received some assistance, however, from members of the Kingston Church, among whom I may mention Daniel L. Wells, Reuben Nichols, John Newhouse, and Harvey Otis—men who have "purchased to themselves a good degree" by their long years of devotion to the Christian cause. I was also aided by the Baptist Church at Sing Sing, which I supplied for several Sabbaths. With these limited resources, I was compelled to live very economically. For nearly two years I united with my room-mate in keeping *bachelors' hall.* The average cost of this enterprise was *three shillings per week each.* Still, our fortunate acquaintance with several good housewives in the village added not a little to our stock of eatables, and we would occasionally vary the bill of fare from the waters of a crystal lake in the neighborhood. All told, our fare was good enough for students, and I have no doubt that if all mankind were to live as we did then, dyspepsia and hypochondria would be unknown.

While I was at work in New York I received a visit from a committee of the Baptist Church in *New Baltimore*, inviting me to become their pastor. I had been gradually reasoning myself into the belief that, the best way to study theology is for a man to take his Bible, and a few good books, and to preach as fast as he learns, and I at once accepted their call. This was in the old *Merchants' Exchange*, alongside of the statue of Alexander Hamilton, who, as I told the brethren, was good enough witness to our contract. The next Sabbath found me at my post, where I was welcomed by a large congregation. After remaining with that church a few months, I was ordained to the work of the ministry, by an *Ecclesiastical Council*, composed of delegates from several neighboring churches.

Some time previous to these events, I had visited my old friend, Rev. Isaac Moore, at Westkill. He gave out an appointment for me to preach in the evening. While discoursing on things divine, my eyes involuntarily rested on a bright-eyed mountain girl, just in front of the pulpit. From the first glance it seemed to me that I could preach better when I was looking that way. To tell the honest truth, I *fell in love with this girl*, and the next day I casually saw her again at her father's house, which only strengthened the sacred passion. Here was "love at first sight," in good earnest. I had seen, and been acquainted with many scores of beautiful young women, but never till then had I felt that peculiar and happy pang which Cupid gives, when he sends his arrow *through and through the heart*. After this I visited Westkill quite frequently. I became quite suddenly, but no less permanently, a complete enthusiast in my admiration of *mountain scenery*, and an ardent disciple of the renowned Isaac Walton (who treats so handsomely on *trout-fishing*), and a great lover of *evening visits*, particularly at the house of Philo Bushnell, Esq., who was father of the young lady referred to—Miss Emeline Bushnell.

I have always tried hard to be a practical man, and to avoid the adoption of visionary and useless theories and sentimentalities. The idea of loving a lady without marrying her, I, at the above period especially, regarded as a piece of great nonsense. Therefore, being most pleasantly situated at New Baltimore—enjoying the favor of the people—having a model boarding-place—and so snugly ensconced in a neat little sanctum, where I sometimes got lonely—I "popped *the* question," and, on the 10th of April, 1836, married the "mountain girl." Since then, I have often heard it from her own lips that Cupid paid her a visit simultaneously with his capers with me. However this may be, I have never regretted my choice, and I am not joking when I recommend this method of getting a wife. The plan adopted by many young men, of searching, and scrutinizing, and courting, and considering, among all the girls in the nation, with a direct view of ascertaining if they can possibly love this, that, or the other one, is most unnatural—for true, and pure, and real "matches" are "made in heaven;" and were I a young lady, and had a thousand hearts to give, not one of them should go to the young gallant who required six months to determine whether he loved me. In one word, matrimony should be an affair of the affections; not a mathematical problem, and much less a matter of dollars and cents. The man who dodges the spirit and design of this holy alliance, by marrying for money, is a wretch, who deserves to be miserable the rest of his days.

Well, blessed with the smiles and counsels of my young bride, I was very happy at New Baltimore. After remaining there a few months longer, I felt it my duty to accept a call from the church at Westkill. Here I continued, as pastor, for *nine years,* during which time I experienced much of the "*Sunny Side,*" as well as the "*Shady Side,*" of that relation. My preaching was *direct* and *plain,* and *designed to cut its way with conscience.* Ever since I have been disabled from preaching, it has been a great consolation to me to reflect that I never "sewed pillows to arm-holes," or "handled the word of God deceitfully." I literally "cried aloud, and spared not," as many can testify, and as my poor throat has been testifying for the last seven years. Had I been as moderate as many of our sleepy sing-songs of the present day, I might have been doling out the Gospel to this day—or I might have been accursed in an early grave, for my indolence, and for my solemn mockeries of the awful themes—I really do not know which. How a man, with vital piety at heart, and a commission from the Great I AM in his hands, and the awful realities of Sin, Death, Hell, Heaven, and a Judgment Day for his themes, and a concourse of eternity-bound immortals before him, can *say over* the Gospel, as a dull boy would say a lesson, is a problem which some of our doctors of divinity would do well to solve.

During my labors in Westkill, the church enjoyed several mighty outpourings of the Holy Spirit. Connected with these, and with my pastorate in general, were many incidents of an interesting character. Most of them I will pass over; the few more particularly connected with the leading events of my history, I may be pardoned for recording.

My salary was very small, never exceeding three hundred dollars; and "donation visits" were not at first in vogue, in this then hot-bed of *antinomianism*—an *ism*, which, of all others, is perhaps least inclined to liberality. This led me to labor with my own hands"—no great condescension, verily, in a minister of the gospel, seeing Paul did the same. I procured printing materials, a good supply of type, and an old "*Ramage Press*," and commenced the publication of a little semi-monthly, called the "*Christian Repository*." I obtained a fair circulation, and realized about $500 profit during its one-year life. Then I abandoned the *first publication ever issued among the Catskill Mountains*, and sent forth the first number of the "*Baptist Library*," a reprint of standard Baptist works, such as those of Bunyan, Keath, Carson, Hall, and Fuller. This idea met with universal sympathy throughout our churches. The first men in the denomination gave me their influence, and at the end of one year I had *seven thousand* subscribers at $1.50 each. My labors between its semi-monthly issues, were about as follows:—

Composition of 16 large pages of type, in which I was aided by wife.
Press-work every fortnight of 7,000 sheets.
Folding, pressing, covering, and mailing 7,000 periodicals every fortnight.
Keeping the books.
Preaching from four to eight sermons.
Attending weddings, funerals, &c.

All told, this was rather hard work, and required full sixteen hours per day. This course made the first inroad on my constitution, and I now regret it most bitterly. I soon found it necessary to enlarge my facilities, when I formed a co-partnership with my brother, R. H. Hill, and we removed our quarters to the delightful village of *Prattsville.* The Hon. Zadock Pratt, founder of that fine village (justly pronounced the "gem of the mountains")—a gentleman well known and highly esteemed throughout the country—became our generous patron, and afforded us the large monied facilities required by our enlarging our operations, in the addition of some *twelve workmen,* a well appointed *stereotype foundry,* and an extensive *book and stationery store.* He also furnished us a large building for our business, and each of us a good house for our families. At the close of the business there—about three years in all—he utterly refused to take any rent. It is not a little to his credit that just such instances of liberality were ever common to him. I remained in Prattsville only about a year, having sold out to my brother, who continued the business some two years after I left. On leaving there, I was resolved to bid adieu to the mountains, and with this view visited Danbury, Conn., Stamford, Conn., and some churches in New Jersey, and returned home to consider and decide on the merits of these several locations. The Westkill church urged me to return, and I did so. After three or four years the famous *anti-rent* troubles commenced. In this section several clergymen lectured for, and otherwise encouraged the *Calico Indians.* I was accused of being an "*up-renter,*" and was threatened with a "donation" suit of "tar and feathers." One day a gang of some eighty of these rowdies passed my house, and while I stood in the door they pointed their muskets at me, but did not fire. Perhaps they were in jest; but even such an outrage no friend of good order would be found guilty of. A sermon in which I plainly exposed the rottenness of the whole system of *disguise,* and the hypocrisy of those professors of religion who countenanced the practice, gave great offence to a few in the church; and being determined not to stay in a church where even a few wished me gone, I left, and settled in the Baptist church in the thriving village of *Saugerties*, on the banks of the Hudson river. There I remained two years and a half, and I must say in justice to the church and the people generally, that my situation was exceedingly pleasant. Indeed I felt as if I could stay in that community "all the days of my life." Alas! it was otherwise ordered. I was severely attacked with that scourge of the ministry, *bronchitis*. At one period of the disease I entirely lost my voice, and such was the aggravated character of the complaint, that skilful physicians pronounced me on the very brink of the consumptive's grave. By the blessing of God, in the free use of "*Jayne's Expectorant*," I almost entirely recovered, and again entered the pulpit. A few sermons were sufficient to bring back the malady in a *chronic form*, and from this I have never entirely recovered. The large quantities of *iodine* and *bromine*, especially the latter, which I was led to use in the practice of daguerreotype, and in manufacturing chemicals, have tended greatly to modify the disease, and to render life endurable. *Bromine*, deadly poison as it is, inhaled by the lungs, in a state of moderate dilution with atmospheric air, appears to act as a tremendous irritant, and for several hours, and even days, the pulmonary subject will feel much worse; but these symptoms are sure to be followed by a very decided improvement. A continuous exposure, however, to even a very weak atmosphere of this poison, is extremely debilitating and injurious. Three years ago the present winter, I had a violent return of my complaint; and about that time I had occasion to make a large quantity of *bromide of lime*. At several different times I inhaled it largely, which caused a very great aggravation of the cough, sore throat, expectoration, stricture, &c., but in a few days the volatile poison left the system, and with it went all the principal symptoms of the disease, and I felt nearly well for several months. A good way to use this potent medicine, is to place *one drop* of pure bromine in a three-gallon jug, and after suffering it to remain corked tight for an hour, in a warm room, to carefully inhale from the mouth of the jug, till you feel a decided action of it through the throat and lungs, *and then to breathe freely out-door air, the colder the better.* The latter direction may seem singular and dangerous, but it is not. No danger of "taking cold" need be apprehended. The lungs are not then in a condition for it. They are under a ten-fold excitement, in the effort to throw off the poison, and will, therefore, resist the cold air, while the latter will at once dilute the gas.

To return to the thread of my narrative. After becoming satisfied that my disease was of a character to forbid my regular exercise of the ministry, I at once turned my attention to *daguerreotyping*. From Daguerre's first published account of this wonderful art, I became enamored with it; and I well remember my emotions on seeing some of the first daguerreotypes made in New York by Prof. Morse (the immortal inventor of the magnetic telegraph), Prof. Wolcott, Mr. Van Loon, and others. I paid one of these gentlemen (Mr. Van Loon, I think) $10 for two medium daguerreotypes of myself and wife. My own, having been kept from strong light, remains on the plate, but in a miserable state of decay; the other has long since entirely disappeared.

My first lessons in daguerreotype were from a friend, who was a novice in the art. Of course I did not succeed. I then repaired to Meade & Brothers' Gallery, in Albany, where I gathered the main principles of the business. Afterwards I spent some time with R. E. Churchill, Esq., in Broadway, New York, much to my improvement. In those days instructions were very imperfectly given; many of the best artists, in fact, found it hard work to keep their own equilibrium, so little was understood of the true principles of the art. After all these valuable aids, I was still in a most woful "fog." My lights had "the blues," and the face of beauty would come out black as charcoal; and that, too, after a sitting of fifteen minutes. Indeed, I thought myself fortunate to make a white man look a few degrees lighter than Jim Crow. To those who have passed through these troubles (and who of the old daguerreotypists have not?), I need not describe their vexations and horrors. The pecuniary embarrassment, likewise, to those who depend on the business for the support of their families, as I did, is no small item. Many—yes, the great majority—who *took instructions* in those days, were wilfully misled, and not only cheated out of their money, but sent out among strangers without the ability to earn their bread. Let me say here, that *certain parties* who have been most forward in denouncing me as a cheat, like themselves, were among the *notorious* in those naughty times, when *cider* was sold for "*quick stuff*," *red chalk* for *colcothar*, *Indian meal* for *chloride of gold*, and *plumbago* for *iodine*. I have the documents to prove this assertion, and I can bring dozens of men who will swear, on the Holy Book, that, in their opinion, the mercenary traducers referred to are among the meanest and most contemptible villains on the footstool. Not a few of these rare spirits I could point out *by name*, and prove their rascality to their teeth; but I will let these remarks suffice, promising, if they ever renew their base attacks, to bring to light *some things which will not be very pleasing*.

In the course of my struggles to gain a mastery of the art, I was one day visited by Mr. Francis Norwood, of Schoharie Co. It was very uncommon in those times to meet with an operator at all *communicative;* every man had some *great secret*, and that was locked up in his own narrow bosom, and the key hid away. You could scarcely visit a daguerreotype room, but you would see on the door of the operating department—"*No Admittance*," "*Positively no Admittance*," "*Strictly Private*," "*Peremptorily no Admittance*," &c. If you desired a piece of information—a recipe for making or mixing "chloride of gold" for example, from $5 to $50 was the price, the seller reserving the trifling privilege of giving you the wrong recipe if he saw fit. I once sent for $5 worth of chloride of gold to a very popular house in Broadway, with a respectful request for information how to mix it. The gold (and plenty of nice *yellow corn*, ground fine) arrived, and with it a message—"Ask Mr. Hill if he thinks I am a d——d fool?" This creature is still on Broadway; but people have found him out, and the glory of his once gorgeous daguerreian palace has departed. I am glad that a race of *men* have taken his place.

Mr. Norwood was of a different stamp. He carried the "key of knowledge" in a loose hand; and he cheerfully "put me on the track." I learned from him, in twenty minutes, that which enabled me to produce very good pictures with some certainty. As a result, I profited to the amount of about four hundred dollars in Saugerties alone, in the space of three or four months. This enabled me to pay all my little debts, contracted while "groping in the dark," and to return to my home in Westkill with a few spare dollars.

Soon after this, accompanied by my wife and boy, I commenced as *travelling daguerreotypist.* I went first of all to the flourishing town of *North East,* Dutchess Co., where I spent a winter very pleasantly in the house of the Rev. H. L. Gross. While there, I made and sold some two hundred pictures. On my return home, I operated for a short time in my native village, Athens. A month or two afterwards I returned to Athens, and had all I could do there for several weeks. Then I went down the river to *Poughkeepsie,* and thence to *Dover Plains,* Dutchess Co., where I was fortunate in forming an extensive acquaintance with most excellent people, and in making and selling nearly three hundred pictures. While there, I enjoyed a visit with Durand, the artist. I naturally supposed that the man who produced the fine painting of *Dover Plains,* could show me how to color a daguerreotype. But he laughed at the idea, remarking, "*reproduce, by means of light, the beautiful colored image on the ground glass of your camera, and you will be ahead of all the painters.*" This remark was, perhaps, what first suggested to me the idea of making an effort towards that grand object.

From Dover Plains I went to the pleasant village of *Amenia,* in the same county, and there, also, I succeeded admirably for a couple of months. I became acquainted while there with the professors in the Methodist Seminary—especially Professors Hazen and Winchell. With them I had many pleasant interviews, the conversation generally turning on the *Philosophy of the Daguerreotype.* In this they were well versed; but the practical part they could not master. The camera, &c., belonging to their Philosophical Department I purchased at a low price, and paid in light and shadow.

In the month of November I returned to *North East,* where I designed to spend the winter; but, in the midst of a most successful career, we were unexpectedly called home by the dangerous illness of a dear sister. We arrived at Oakhill, opposite Catskill, on our way homeward, after dark the first day. The river had just closed, but the crossing not being safe, we went up to Hudson, and crossed there, piloted by two little boys, and arrived at Catskill at midnight. The next morning, at daybreak, we were on our way to the mountains. It was one of the coldest days I ever knew, and in crossing the mountain, just below the "Mountain House," the wind blew a perfect hurricane. The air was literally filled with snow, leaves, limbs of trees, and an occasional sprinkling of rails and boards from the fences, and several times we heard the crash of tall maples and hemlocks, as they yielded to the fury of the gale. Majesty rode on the blast that day. I name this incident, because it formed a sort of era in my life, and to show what *woman* can endure, when on a mission of affection. Several times we were plunged into deep snow drifts, when my wife, our little boy, and myself had to release the prancing and infuriated steeds, right up the sleigh, or tumble it over a stone wall, and play vigilance committee over the stupid acts of an affrighted *negro driver.*

Arrived safely home, we found our young friend, to all appearance, in the last agonies of a complication of diseases, of which *Scrofula* was chief. She had been given up by several physicians, and had been lying for some days in a comatose state. We were aware that she had taken the usual remedies of the Allopathic school, and having reached the end of their *medical education,* it was considered that any new prescription, not exactly conforming to these principles, would kill her at once. However we, in theory and practice, were *Thompsonians*—the mention of which fact here needs no apology—for the *theory* of Dr. Samuel Thompson never has, and never can be refuted, though the course of some of his followers has been utterly absurd. Accordingly, by consent of the entire family, we made a trial of botanic remedies. Small doses of Thompson's *Third Preparation,* to get up the "*internal heat,*" and *nauseate the stomach,* were often repeated, aided by a careful and persevering use of the *vapor bath.* The effect was almost magical. Signs of life began to appear, and ere long *she was in great pain.* As soon as we thought it safe we gave, *to relieve these pains, the same medicine,* in *emetic doses.* Nature, thus aided, gained strength to renew the conflict with disease; and the advantage was followed up by a continued use of the same medicine, in connexion with *vegetable alteratives,* till the patient recovered. She is still living in the enjoyment of fair health.

I have said that the journey through the hurricane was a sort of *era* in my life. How and why I so regard it I will now state. Had we been one day later our friend, I doubt not, would have died, and we would have returned to our migrations. As it was, duty retained me at home, and having no regular employment *I began experimenting for the natural colors.* These experiments I have continued till very recently—a period of over five years—and had it not been for the heroic fortitude of a woman, in braving the storm, the following pages would never have seen the light.

I will not omit, in this place, the mention of some unpleasant circumstances which happened about this time. The then Pastor of the Westkill church had been guilty of most shamefully slandering one of the most amiable young ladies in the place. Unfortunately for me he had made me a witness to the fact, and though I deemed it prudent to conceal my knowledge of his character, supposing that there was no other proof, the whole thing leaked out, and it was proved against him by the most irrefragable testimony. He was tried by a council of delegates from ten or twelve neighboring churches, excluded from the church, and silenced from preaching by the unanimous finding of the council. During the progress of the matter this man tried hard to injure me, and to effect his purpose set on foot a shameful lie. This I at once traced out, and in a few days caused to be read in public two *libels*, signed by the parties implicated; and thus the matter ended until some of my spiteful *natural color friends* repeated the story. These *friends*, made malicious by their failure to browbeat me into a compliance with their wishes in regard to my discovery, had the pleasure, for a short time, of being believed. Several, to my knowledge, on visiting Westkill and making the most diligent inquiry, both here and on the road, were quite thunderstruck to find that not even a shadow of suspicion existed against me. This is the first time I ever named the subject in print, and I do it now as a matter of history, without feeling any interest in the matter, or any special concern about the opinions of the *very kind friends* referred to.

When I commenced working for the colors I had a little, and but a little, faith. As I progressed I noticed things that greatly increased my confidence in the practicability of what I regarded as the true *chromatic theory*. Not that I produced any *colors*, but I found that ordinary Daguerreotyping and Calotyping, with slight variations, were capable of giving very great diversity of tone; and I found, also, that other agents besides the usual ones would give singular and sometimes beautiful results. This led me on from day to day, and gave me great encouragement to believe that I would one day find an opening that would lead me into the *Land of the Beautiful*. The great difficulty was to find a *clue* to some mode of operating *direct* for the colors. This secured, the next difficulty was in procuring *suitable chemicals*. I found, on personal inquiry at the best Laboratories in the United States, that many of my supplies would have to come from *Europe*. Then I began to open my eyes to the fact that experimenting was *very costly*,* and that my means would soon be gone.

At this time *no book on the Daguerreotype Art had ever been published in this country*, and I had long been collecting materials for such a work. I had paid out several hundred dollars for recipes, &c., and at length, with fear and trembling, I issued proposals for my "*Treatise on Daguerreotype.*" The circular was inadvertently dated the *First of April*, and I soon had several letters inquiring if I meant to *April-fool* the fraternity. One of these letters was from a distinguished operator in Philadelphia, with whom I have since had many a laugh over the subject. He could not believe that a proposal to publish a *Book on Daguerreotype* could be less than an *April-fooling*. Imperfect as my first work certainly was, it met with a ready sale at $5 per copy, and it was thought quite cheap enough at that price, inasmuch as it contained, in addition to a full system of operating, many recipes which had frequently sold for from $10 to $50 each, and much other valuable information. I realized a few hundred dollars profits from the sale of this work, which made me feel quite rich, and enabled me to push my experiments.

In the meantime I took daguerreotypes for all who called, and occasionally had a *pupil*. My price for teaching a pupil was $50, which some persons, *who never do it for less*, have charged upon me as a piece of extortion. The truth is just this: I always spent from one to two months with a pupil, and carefully taught him every branch of the art; and I have never yet had one leave my rooms who was not qualified to make money out of the business. All of them, as far as I know, have done well; and many of them are now among the best and most successful operators in the country. Not one of them ever grumbled at my treatment, and *all* of them are, to this day, among my warmest friends. These remarks I design to apply to all the pupils I ever had, and the reader may judge from them how far I am

* To this date I have spent over *ten thousand dollars* in these experiments.

guilty of depredating upon their credulity. I would not refer to this subject, were it not that many unkind insinuations have been thrown out concerning it, as if it was a great privilege for me to labor like a slave in teaching my scholars, *for the very purpose* of purchasing the boon of working for that which could but benefit the whole fraternity. *Every dollar* ever received from pupils, books, the sale of chemicals, &c., has been spent, long since, in the *pursuit of my experiments*. Any persons who may feel sufficient interest in my *private affairs* (for such they certainly are) will be referred to my many former pupils by name, to many persons of distinction who are acquainted with my affairs, and to any of my neighbors within ten or twenty miles of my house.

I would state, further, that I have published, besides the present volume, *four works on Photography :*

1. My original *Treatise on Daguerreotype.*
2. A *revised* and *enlarged edition of the same.*
3. A Treatise on the "*Magic Buff*," &c.
4. "*Photographic Researches and Manipulations.*

The "Treatise on the Magic Buff" was a pamphlet merely, and sold for *five dollars* to all who saw fit to buy it. This speculation brought down upon me a tirade of abuse in a certain city paper, written by a man who has since not hesitated to attack one of the most venerable institutions in our country—the *Franklin Institute.*

At the time I projected that *pamphlet* "*Magic Buffs*" were selling for twenty dollars per pair. They were simply two pieces of buckskin tacked to pine sticks, one strip of the buckskin having a *little grease* spread over its surface. As respectable parties as the Scovill Manufacturing Co., W. & W. H. Lewis, J. Gurney, and others, were in the speculation ; and there was no unfairness in it—for, by the use of these Buffs the Daguerreotype plate was quickened *one half,* thus enabling operators to take children and other difficult subjects with great facility. I purchased three sets of the Buffs, and there being no patent on them, I had wit enough to analyse one of them. Those who sold the *pieces of leather* and the *pine sticks* for twenty dollars did not give *the secret.* My logic was as follows: *Two pine sticks covered with buckskin strips, one of them greased,* are worth twenty dollars—therefore, the grand *modus* of preparing the said buckskin, &c., is worth five dollars. My *subscribers,* as far as I know, agreed with me that I hit logic's nail on the head that time. I had the lion's share of the profits —some $500—and the gratification also of somewhat out-generaling my New York friends fairly, handsomely, and in a nice business way. The information becoming general, buckskin fell in price, and Dr. Cyrus (the reputed inventor) was relieved of all danger of being burned for witchcraft. So much for the famous "*Magic Buff.*"

My other publications (a thousand thanks to the great mass of my brother artists) went off at a profit, especially the "*Photographic Researches,*" which sold freely throughout the United States, in the Canadas, and to some extent in Europe. I wrote the book as over-work, at midnight hours—at a time, too, when my mind was on the pinnacle of excitement about the natural colors. At midnight hours also I wrote and mailed my Prospectus; and having thus, by my own efforts, secured the kind patronage of the fraternity, I think I was, and am, justly entitled to commendation instead of blame, especially as I spent all the money in pursuit of the grandest theme of Photography, and especially as I can show *one thousand letters* from actual subscribers, expressing their high appreciation of the work. A few weeks ago I sold, for a liberal price, the copy-right of this work to one of the first stock dealers in the country—Myron Shew, Esq., of Philadelphia.

My reader is now made aware of pretty much the whole story concerning the manner in which I have sustained my family, and my experiments for the last five years. I would add, however, that I have realized moderate profits from the sale of Daguerreotype and Calotype chemicals of my own make, and Daguerreotype stock. After *earning* and *spending* over *ten thousand dol-*

lars, and at the end of five years of the severest toils, brain-racking investigations, and *bitter trials*, I find myself a few hundred dollars worse than a poor man. I am aware that the impression is abroad that I have amassed an immense fortune. One writer has taken pains to figure up my gains, and he made out about *forty thousand dollars*. But the whole truth is given in the foregoing statements, with the exception of the fact that the *very house I live in, and of which I hold a deed, has been under mortgage for three years past.* The money for which the mortgage was given was, every dollar of it, expended in my experiments. My neighbors are perfectly familiar with these facts, and I consider them as a full vindication against all insinuations to the contrary.

CHAPTER II.

Experimenting—Difficulties in the Way—Groping in Darkness—Friends Laugh—The Philosophers—Wife Aids—Laughable Experiments—Wife has the Consumption—A peculiar mode of Treatment, by which her life was greatly prolonged, briefly detailed—Poisons—Explosions—Friendly Cautions—The first Picture in Colors—Excitement of Mind—Second Picture in Colors—The Announcement—Effect on the Public Mind—Injury to the Daguerreotype Business—Eight thousand Letters—Visitors—Speculators—Offers of large sums of Money—The Press—Course of the Photographic Journals—The "Infernal Committee"—Life Threatened—My Revolver—Its Amusing History—Col. Pratt's Dog—The Midnight Alarm—Narrow Escape of the Enemy—Westkill Police—Watchman's Rattle—Friends—M. A. Root, Wm. M. Marshall, Prof. Morse, and others—Visitors and Visitations—Glass Silvering—$5,000 turning on a piece of India-rubber Cloth—Reflectors for Cameras—The Pantotype—Beautiful method of making Daguerreotype Plates—The Chromatint, fully detailed—My Second Marriage—A piece of unlooked for Experience—That "foulest whelp of sin," Slander—Human Nature in its blackest apparel.

In the midst of toils of which the foregoing chapter gives but a meagre account, I pursued my grand theme—my *one thought*, so to speak—and never, for a wakeful hour, whatever else might be on my hands, did I cease to *think into it*. It was like studying arithmetic on a battle field—like balancing on the tight-rope in a tornado—like anything but the usual method of scientific pursuit. Say it was like Thomas Scott, writing a commentary, with a cross baby on his knee. That will do—a tolerable figure of the plight I was in.

At first I was *alone—all alone*—a sort of human owl, grubbing about, with great blurry eyes, after a glow-worm. My acquaintances—my best friends—brothers, sisters, wife—all laughed at me. To them, doubtless, I seemed like one fishing for pearls in a thunder cloud. My scheme was ranked with "*perpetual motion*" hunting. In one word, I was a *visionary*, a builder of *air-castles*. This, as you may readily imagine, was not very encouraging. I referred them to *facts*, *phenomena*, *chromatic theory*, and the like; but it was of no use, like the rest of mankind they had set the thing down among the *impossibilities*. I should tell a lie to say that this conduct on their part did not mortify my pride exceedingly. However, I will give them all credit of having refrained from harshness. It was a sort of stationary theme in the family for cracking jokes over. I would try to smile and laugh in a natural way—but I was like the frogs in the fable—the boys' fun in stoning them, was their agony.

This *utter unbelief* in the possibility of solving the great problem, was not confined to my family. It was, as far as men thought on the subject, a well-settled *public sentiment*. I do not think I could have found a man or woman who would have ventured five dollars on my success. The scientific minds of this country and Europe, with a few brilliant exceptions, even went so far as *to take it for granted* that *photography* and the *natural colors* were separated by an impassable gulf. The *old philosophers* had never had their giant minds enlisted in the subject. Hence I had no help from *the books*.

Another great impediment was my *lack of chemical knowledge*. True, I had *read* the science in school, and I could *recite* its outlines; but I had never *studied* it. To *study chemistry* in the true sense, is to *practise* it. In my attempts to make my own chemicals, I found myself wofully deficient. In following the plainest formulas I frequently failed. Of *apparatus* I had none. Even now, after years of practice, I have very little in this line but what I have made myself. They answer my purpose. My methods of forming and compounding are mostly my own. The formulas in this work are not all given in true chemical technicality; but I have tried hard to be *plain* and *correct*.

After a few months my wife became a convert to my views, and entered heartily into my spirit and plans. We worked together with untiring perseverance. Every variety of experiment that our anxious thoughts suggested, was tried in every form, and repeated, over and over again, until we were satisfied that it did not contain our sought-for gem. Knowing as I *now* do, the almost impossibility of avoiding, in such a research, certain absurd acts, and queer juxtapositions, I am yet amused in looking back at some of our experiments. True, we had a sort of *system*, and usually confined ourselves to one head of the series at a time. Under the head of "*Mordants*," for example, we one day applied *alum water* to a plate, and then coated it in the usual way with iodine, thinking that in some way the *alumina*, which has a great affinity to *coloring matter*, might lay hold of the colored rays. This was absurd enough, truly; but, as it cost but little time, there was no harm done, and it led in the end to the employment of *aluminate of silver*, as you will see further on. Indeed, out of the many thousand experiments I have tried, I do not remember a single one from which I derived no benefit.

My wife's devotion to the pursuit lasted several months. Many of her ideas and manipulations were excellent—such as only woman could originate. Household duties called her away from the work, and I afterwards enjoyed her aid only occasionally. Her exertions in this work, and exposure to noxious chemicals, I fear had a share in hastening the development of her present hereditary disease. At the time of this writing, she lies low under the hand of that fell destroyer—*consumption*. My own health has suffered greatly, from the ardor of my labors, and from the many deadly poisons which have been, as it were, my playthings for years. Such inhalants as prussic acid, phosphorus, sulphuretted hydrogen, cyanogen, nitrous oxide, chlorine, bromine, red hot arsenic, antimony, &c., are not exactly suited to the frail net-work of the human lungs. Once in particular, after the continued use of hydrofluoric acid, I had a severe attack of hemorrhage of the lungs, and was very singularly handled. I have also had many hair-breadth escapes from *explosions*. Having occasion one day to prepare some *fulminate of silver*, an explosion took place which shook the whole premises, and though I was within five feet of the vile stuff, not a hair of my head was injured. At another time I was knocked over, as if with a club, by the fumes of prussic acid, *which I was heroically heating on a plate*, with, as I thought, requisite precautions. More than once I have been *etherealized*, *iodized*, *bromidized*, *oxydized*, *chloroformed*, and, in various other ways, *transformed* from the natural to a most unnatural state. These injuries were most of them *temporary;* worse ones have arisen from *continued* exposure to volatile poisons, lack of out-door exercise, late hours, over exertion of the physical and mental powers, and a tremendous and lengthened excitement of the mind. May future experimenters who read these lines take warning from my example. Let me say to those who *galvanize their plates*, beware of your *cyanide of silver*—its fume contains a poison subtle as, and *almost identical with*, that of the *rattle-snake*. Keep it in a distant corner, and give it ventilation. When not in use, let it be well covered. Beware, also, of your *bromine*—the very rottenness of death is in it. Ventilate your mercury—its fume is loaded with rheumatism, sciatica, lumbago, tooth-ache, neuralgia, and decrepitude. Beware of air-tight rooms, close confinement, standing, sitting, stooping too much, reading too much, too much eating, too little sleep, too much abstraction of mind, and too much of any bad habit whatever. Let King Philip's motto be posted on all your employments—"*Remember thou art mortal*." Lost health is not easily regained. Receive this friendly admonition from one who knows, by bitter experience, the fruits of violating the laws of physiology and hygiene.

It was in the spring of 1847 that I commenced these experiments. For three entire years I obtained no really encouraging result. True, I occasionally saw some remarkable change in the *tone* of ordinary daguerreotype and calotype pictures, as I varied these processes—some striking freak in the chemical or actinic action—for example, the *red* figures in a dress or building, or tints of *green* in a landscape dimly showing themselves. The same phenomenon was early noticed by Daguerre, and has been frequently observed by others. Sometimes I would obtain an *iridescent play of colors,* such as we see in thin plates of mica, mother-of-pearl, the soap-bubble, &c.; but these I knew were due to a cause foreign to that I was striving to bring into action, that is, they were not the result of actinic power.

My first really good result was obtained in 1850. It was a copy of a large colored lithograph of the village of Prattsville. Never, before or since, did I experience such overpowering mental excitement as when I saw this result. Wearied and worn with the toils of three long years, I was, as it were, suddenly ushered into a place of repose and beauty. My brain reeled and staggered under the mighty fact that I had reached the goal of my hopes, and I shouted, like a Methodist—*Eureka! Eureka!* It seemed to me that the house was too small to hold my suddenly expanded thoughts, and I made my way to a clump of "willows," near a running brook, where, Ophelia-like, I soliloquized all manner of sentimentalism, and employed myself for an hour or two, in the important business of picking up, and tossing about the pebbles on the water's edge. To my entranced gaze, every stone, and leaf, and even each of my hands, had a heliochrome upon it. Indeed, I was, for the only time in my life, on the verge of insanity. Suddenly, the thought struck me that I must make a desperate effort to *remember* how I had secured that picture. Having used no definite proportions in my compounds, I found it necessary to make a desperate effort to remember the quantities of each material employed, by calling up to my mind, by a sort of mnemonics, the form and bulk of the articles. I accordingly locked myself in my room, and went to work deliberately to *construct a formula.* In the nature of the case this effort was the keystone of my future success.

I succeeded in producing *a second picture in natural colors.* To me, and to my wife, this was a thrilling event. Then it was that we signed and made oath to a pledge, which afterwards gave me much trouble. This pledge we designed for our own security, and its binding obligation formed the reason for my refusal to show my pictures, "except for security or protection." This refusal led many to suspect that the whole thing was a pretence; but never in my life have I acted more conscientiously than I did in religiously adhering to this pledge.

Having made so great a discovery, was it not natural, and reasonable, and *proper*, for me to *announce* it? For so doing I have been severely censured; inasmuch as the excitement which followed greatly injured the daguerreotype business—a result I had little dreamed of. In making that announcement I did no more than to act out of the natural impulsiveness of my own nature. Its effect I did not foresee. This effect was most unexpected to me. None will deny that it exceeded any parallel case in this country. The news spread like wild-fire. Every newspaper in the land contained glowing accounts of the matter—everybody talked about it—and the Daguerreotype business received a mighty blow. No person ever regretted this more than I have; but *it was not wrong in me, under the circumstances, to make that announcement.* The *Editors of our own Photographic Journals,* who first *announced* (all very right), and then, in a way of provoking, unfair, and long-spun controversy, *denounced* my discovery, and most unrighteously, and with a sort of "border-ruffian" spirit, abused and vilified me, are the men who inflicted the "unkindest cut of all" on the bleeding body of Daguerreanism. To them the Press at large naturally looked for information, and their editorials, *for* and *against,* were eagerly copied. Justice to myself compelled me to counteract their unmanly scandals, by means of "certificates" from men of note to whom I exhibited the proofs of my own integrity. Is a man blameworthy for defending himself from the attacks of scribbling, literary bloodhounds? If so, then have I offended.

I, of all others, have been the greatest sufferer from that *announcement.* One result was the reception of over *eight thousand letters.* No small affliction for a man employed. Another result was a "great multitude" of visitors, and not a few "visitations." No less an affliction was the officious intermeddling of a certain class of sharpers and speculators, who left no effort untried to get me involved in their expert clutches. Some of them, when at length they found out I was not quite a fool, fell back on the tricks of old traitor Judas, and circulated all manner of lies, to my hurt.

The "*Committee*" of the miserable apology for a "New York State Daguerrean Association," who visited me during this stage of the proceedings, well illustrated, in their course, the character of that justice which I received. The whole history of this "Infernal Committee" affair may be told in a few words. It is this:—Three men—D. D. T. Davy, "Phot." of Utica, Clark of New York, and Tomlinson of Troy—came to my house, under orders from the mighty compact referred to—the "N. Y. State Daguerrean Association"—whose mandate issued from a meeting of said august body, in a Daguerrean Gallery in New York, which meeting was composed of a tremendous gathering of no less than *seven members*—yea, verily, and *no more* than seven. This "Committee" (in justice to Tomlinson and Clark, I would say) was made up, *de facto*, of the notorious Davy. He was chief speaker—the two others being evidently ashamed of their connexion with so mean and dastardly a spirit as that exhibited by their chairman. This Davy, after a liberal effusion of flattery, and after a kind reception from me, proceeded to threaten me with exposure as a humbug, and more than intimated that a banditti of ruffians, like himself, would visit this quiet valley with the laudable purpose of *breaking into my laboratory*. Surely, no two threats could be more *contradictory*. One supposed I had no pictures, and the other implied that I held the key to a gem worthy of the arts and efforts of freebooters. I could have had the chivalrous "Phot." arrested for threatening my life; but I thought the best thing I could do for my neighbors was to let him vamose the valley as quickly as possible.

I candidly confess that I was afraid of the threatened attack.

Davy's whole manner was that of a desperado, and his subsequent history proves that my estimate of his character proves correct. He has since been adjudged by a Court of Arbitration, guilty of *perjury* and *arson*, in the matter of the burning of his Daguerrean Rooms.

I have ever been a man of peace—but I felt that a deep and deadly malice lurked in the dark bosoms of the Davy party, and I accordingly prepared for war. My first step was to procure a *Revolver;* secondly, Col. Pratt sent me one of his watch-dogs; and thirdly, my neighbors organized what I have called the "Westkill Police." The latter consisted of neighboring farmers, and others, who held themselves ready, at a moment's warning, to come to the rescue. The understanding was, that in case of an attack we were to sound a "watchman's rattle," which was kindly furnished me by a Philadelphia friend. All told, we had quite a formidable arrangement, and the Bully Davy and his cowardly satellites would have acquired some experience in the "least refrangible" of the "natural colors," had they ventured an attempt at executing their threat. In other words—the dog would have inserted his ivory daggers into their veins, the revolver would have enlarged the openings, and our mountain boys would have well acted their part in the play of "catching a Tartar." The threat made by Davy had produced a feeling of indignation throughout this whole community; and I say, in all seriousness, that it is well the redoubtable "Phot" chose the "better part of valor."

One dark night we were alarmed by the terrific barking of the faithful dog. I immediately arose from bed, and after listening for a few moments at one of the doors, I became satisfied that the enemy was around. There was a tramping, and a strange crawling noise, and a sort of harsh, grazing sound, as if hoarse voices were plotting for a deed "without a name." I felt sure that the villains were about commencing their work, and such was my indignation that I forgot all about the "rattle," and the thought of summoning the "*Police*" did not enter my mind. The dog put in his high notes, after a fashion I had never heard in dog before. I was well paid for my fright and excitement by what I learned that night of the nature of the canine race. Such yelping, barking, and howling, such tiger fierceness, and savage ferocity, and such an uncontrollable anxiety to get at his prey, was surely never surpassed by dog before. As the noise out of doors did not abate, notwithstanding the terrors of that dog's voice, I really began to have quite an exalted idea of "Phot's" bravery.

Gentle reader, have patience, and I will tell you the sequel. I am aware that in reading stories of great battles, the reader is naturally anxious to come to that point where the bugle sounds the charge, and he can hear the booming thunder of the cannon, and the crash of arms, and see the tide of battle set in and decide the contest. Therefore, to keep you no longer from this thrilling point in my story, I will state the interesting fact, that, with no other soldier but the dog, I opened the door, and rushed upon the enemy—when, lo and behold, instead of meeting the chivalrous "Phot" and his ruffian army—instead of having a chance to display our valor, and to spit out the fire of our patriot souls—we encountered *our old cow*—which discovery the dog and I both made at once. It is quite unnecessary for me to waste words in informing the reader that I felt "sold," and that the dog returned to his station with his tail pointed downwards towards the Chinese Empire.

Lightly as I have treated this item in my history, I assure the reader that I was seriously afflicted by this shameful affair. It formed one link in a chain of annoyances—not a very short chain, either. One of the keenest inflictions a sensitive nature can endure, is to feel that a complication of cruel and unjust proceedings are gathering, like storm-clouds, around our pathway. This, I could easily show, was my situation; but I will draw a curtain on the dark scene, and let my enemies, and their nefarious ideas of right and wrong, sink into that broad immensity of contempt where all such *things* go. Amid all these trials I had a large circle of friends. My neighbors were very kind to me, and the number of warm friends I found in the photographic circle would have to be counted by hundreds and thousands. Among the latter class, who were early by my side, and who have stood by me through "evil and good report," I will mention Marcus A. Root, Esq., and Wm. M. Marshall, Esq., Philadelphia, C. C. Harrison, optician, New York, and Prof. S. F. B. Morse, inventor of the magnetic telegraph. From these gentlemen, who have been familiar with my experiments, I have received invaluable counsel and encouragement. Their names, with those of many others, are graven upon my heart's best affections.

During my long years of incarceration within the walls of my laboratory I have brought out several other inventions. Among the number I will name the following:

I. A GLASS SILVERING PROCESS.

This is now in the hands of the "American Glass Silvering Co.," New York. It is a process for depositing pure silver on glass, and is justly ranked among the gems of art. This invention I sold for the *inappropriate* sum of $5,000. It is worth to-day, $500,000. The adaptation of India rubber cloth to this process, for the purpose of holding the glass articles to be silvered, was its salvation. My $5,000, inadequate as it was, turned on a piece of *Vulcanized Rubber*. Without this, the process could not be used for unequal or large surfaces. Among the applications of the process, the fabrication of *Camera Reflectors* is not the least. No other reflector half as good as these was ever made.

II. THE PANTOTYPE;

A method of securing a *universal focus*. By its means a portrait can be taken with a landscape background, and groups of any number may be produced with perfect sharpness. I have greatly simplified this process, of late, entirely dispensing with the use of the expensive concave mirror.

III. A BEAUTIFUL METHOD OF MAKING DAGUERREOTYPE PLATES.

I silver a plate glass, by means of the process above named, and thicken this by precipitating copper upon it by the electrotype, and then detach the plate from the glass. The process is simple and certain, and the plates of very superior quality.

IV. THE CHROMATINT.

This is a method of coloring Engravings and Photographs. The effect is magnificent, and any person of common skill can work the process. The engraving is rendered transparent by means of a varnish, made by dissolving Gum Damar in turpentine. It is then colored in oil on its back by a system of *daubing*. The effect on the face of the picture is really beautiful. The varnish is easily made, by dissolving 1lb. of Gum Damar in one quart of Spirits of Turpentine, by the aid of heat. A little Camphor Gum added to it renders it less liable to crack. It is first rubbed into the back of the picture, and then floated on its face until the paper is rendered transparent. The colors used are the common oil colors.

V. THE ALCOHOL PROCESS.

By means of which I procure alcohol direct from its *gaseous elements*. The cost of manufacture will not exceed *ten cents* per gallon. I shall bring this discovery before the public at an early day.

VI. A NEW LIGHT—

Far exceeding in brilliancy the ordinary gas-light—perfectly safe and simple, and cheaper than tallow candles. This is my latest invention, and I am now busy in preparing it for public inspection and sale. All who have seen it agree that it will supersede the ordinary gas-light at once, and that no other plan for a "*Portable Light*" will at all compare with it. The light is *perfectly white*, from its base up, emits no smell or smoke, is soft and pleasing to the eye, and yields much more light than any other device. The trouble of keeping it in working order is no more per day than that of trimming one oil lamp. It entirely does away with all the terrors of *camphene*, vaporized hydro-carbons, and "noisome" odor of the ordinary gas-light, with the impositions and cheats of gas companies, and is beautifully adapted to *family use, hotels, factories, churches, street lights, stores, shops*, &c. &c.

I now return to a subject of most painful interest to my feelings—viz. the sickness and death of the companion of my youth. For two entire years she writhed under the agonies of that terrific malady—*the consumption*. In the circular I promised to give a "peculiar method of treatment by which her life was greatly prolonged," and, I may add, her pathway to the cold grave greatly smoothed, and freed from the pangs and horrors of that thorny way. The method consisted of four parts. 1. The warm bath, as often as every other day, and sponging off with cold alcohol, and friction with a crash towel. 2. A drink of the tea of *black alder bark, yellow dock, prince's pine, the twigs of white pine, burdock root* and *sarsaparilla*. These articles were infused in *warm*, not *hot* water—the tea strained and cooled—and used constantly, *without any other drink*. 3. *Inhalants*—not Hunter's *iodide of ethyle* (this she tried to her sorrow), but tepid infusions of herbs and roots. In the selection of the articles I was guided by her symptoms. If her cough was dry I used *hoarhound, boneset, lobelia, liquorice*,

Iceland moss, and other expectorants and demulcents. If there was too free expectoration, I used *elecampane*, *red raspberry leaves*, *witch hazel bark*, *bayberry bark*, and other astringents. For anodyne effect, I used *poppies*, *wild lettuce*, *valerian*, &c. 4. Particular attention was paid to the *extremities*. If they became cold I used bottles of hot water, applied to the feet, hands, and spine. By keeping the bottles on that portion of the spine opposite the distress in the lungs, I generally succeeded in producing a lull of the pain, and great relief to the constricted state of the chest, which was an invariable attendant of cold extremities.

The relief afforded by these simple means was an astonishment to neighbors and physicians who were familiar with the case. I will further remark, that these, or any other means, are useless unless *persevered in*. Being simple and harmless in themselves, they may be freely and continuously applied without the slightest harm. If these statements shall lead to the use of this simple plan, by even one poor consumptive, I shall be amply repaid for the risk I run of being charged with a palpable digression.

Alas! Alas! after all my pains, and my two years' hard toil, by night and by day, I was doomed to see the final triumph of the relentless malady. My agony, and that of my children, in that hour when remedies lost their virtue, when the yearnings of natural affection became vain, and when the pallor of death overspread those loved features, I will not attempt to depict. Neither will I refer to the gloom, and loneliness, and withering blight of every earthly joy, which followed this affliction. Those only who experience, can realize the feelings of a family thus bereaved!

The following notice of this sad event appeared in the *New York Chronicle*. It was written by her pastor and mine, Rev. A. E. Clark.

"Emeline B. Hill. Died, at Westkill, Greene Co., New York, March 23, Mrs. Emeline B. Hill, the beloved wife of Rev. L. L. Hill, aged thirty-eight years.

"At an early period of her life, Sister Hill became the subject of soul-saving religious impressions, put on Christ by immersion, and became attached to the Baptist Church, of which she remained a member, till summoned to join the triumphant ranks of the general assembly and church of the first-born before the throne.

"Her last sickness was severe and protracted. For many months she was pining and wasting away, and all the streams of vitality within her gradually failing, under the relentless influence of deadly consumption, in its worst, its most inveterate form. When she became fully conscious of her situation, and felt herself within the grasp of a disease which would never relax its hold upon her frame till it had brought her to the house appointed for all the living, she bowed in submission to the will of heaven, commended her family to the care of a covenant-keeping God, and calmly and peacefully awaited the final issue, assured that death would be her eternal gain, and that when absent from the body she should be present with the Lord. When the hour of her departure arrived, she was fully prepared to welcome the King of Terrors with a smile; and with the unclouded eye of faith could see the pearly gates unfolded, and the heavenly charioteers who waited to waft her emancipated spirit to its home in the skies. Resting with implicit confidence upon the atoning sacrifice of Christ, and upon the promises of the gospel, death, to her, was bereft of its sting, and her end unalloyed peace.

"It must be gratifying to all connected with our departed sister, to know that everything that human and Christian affection could do to alleviate her sufferings, soothe her mind, and soften her dying pillow, was cheerfully and assiduously done. Our bereaved brother, moved by the promptings of warm affection and deep sympathy towards a suffering and dying wife, suspended experiments which possessed an interest of the deepest intensity to his mind, arising from the discoveries which he had made, and the pursuit of which had almost become an indispensable necessity of his nature, and for long months of deep anxiety devoted himself unremittingly as a minister to her wants and wishes. A large circle of relatives and friends also stood ready at all times, by offices of kindness, to give practical and palpable evidence of the sympathies of their hearts.

"The Baptist Church in Westkill mourn another sad breach made in their ranks; but rejoice in the confidence that their loss has added to the number of those who compose the family above." A. E. C.

The wearisome months that followed this heavy blow, I will pass over in silence. Suffice it to say, that after a period of suffering which pen cannot describe, I resolved on availing myself of the beneficent provisions of nature, as an antidote to my griefs. God himself hath said, "*It is not good for man to be alone.*" My eminently social nature required a place to repose itself—my affections needed a "place of habitation"—and I committed the *crime of a second marriage.* On the 28th of November, 1855, I married Miss Ellen Webber, daughter of Henry Webber, Esq., Greenville, Greene Co., New York. Had I not thought her to be "*the fairest among women,*" as King Solomon expresses it, I would have looked farther. To reveal the whole truth—I adopted the old-fashioned plan of marrying for love, and not for policy, and I acted on the awful assumption, that I had a perfect right to marry whom and when I pleased, albeit the officious intermeddling and "match-making" propensities of my acquaintances. "This was the head and front of my offending." But for this, my unparalleled impudence, I have been subjected to a "course of treatment" quite sufficient to medicate any one mind with a full knowledge of "*human nature in its blackest apparel.*"

I used to think I understood human nature; but I was quite mistaken. I never graduated in the science until the past winter. Now I have my *diploma*, and though I would not be egotistical, I will say, that I consider myself fully qualified to *diagnose* a *Judas neighbor*, a *hypocritical friend*, a *gossiping, gabbling circle of mischief-making women*, and the charms of that state of society in which large numbers are skilled in the highly respectable art of attending to everybody's business but their own, and wofully deficient in that occupation whose poetry is—

"Trouble your head with your own affairs."

Nothing is more provoking than to be made the subject of unfounded gossip, unless it is to witness the perfidy and hollow-heartedness of those we have regarded as confidential friends, in becoming one of the parties to scandal; for it is an old and true saying—"It takes two to make a slander: one to tell it, and one to listen to it." These things are still more aggravating when they exist in those who are indebted to us for important services. And when, after the tattling race-course has had its run, to have those self-same traitors come marching around, for a renewal of intercourse, with the lie on their lips that they meant no harm, is rather too much for a man who knows what truth, decency, law, and gospel are. I have had some "unlooked for" experience in these things; but thank God, I have been blessed with the counsels and smiles of one who is to me as a "guardian angel," and I have been kept from resentment when I had it in my power to punish severely.

On the whole, I can say with another, "Why should a living man complain?" Notwithstanding the ills of this world, I love to live in it. It is a place of beauty; it is filled with delights; it has ten thousand sources of enjoyment; and none of them, perhaps, aside from religion itself, are superior to those joys which grow on the tree of science. And now, after nine years devoted application to the pursuit of "hidden things," I cannot say that I look back on my course with a single regret, except what arises from my own deficiencies.

Kind reader—may you and I be found filling our stations and improving our talents for the good of our race; may it be said of us that we lived in the world without hurting it; and when death shall summon us to eternal scenes, may we have an abiding hope in the Redeemer of sinners, and go to dwell in the "house not made with hands," eternal in the heavens.

L. L. Hill.

Westkill, Greene Co., New York, June 15, 1856.

TREATISE ON HELIOCHROMY.

CHAPTER I.

Light—Various Theories—Atomic and Wave Theories—Properties of Light —Actinic Principle in Light—The Photogenic Ray.

SEVERAL theories have been advanced respecting the nature and propagation of light; but as only two of them have commanded the general attention of philosophical minds, I will confine my remarks to these.

1. The *Corpuscular View.* This supposes that light is composed of particles, of excessive minuteness, projected from the luminous body with a velocity equal to nearly 200,000 miles in a second. This was Sir Isaac Newton's hypothesis. Till recently, it has been agreed to by the great majority of opticians.

2. The *Wave* or *Undulating Theory* regards light as an ethereal fluid of great elasticity; propagated from luminous bodies with inconceivable rapidity. The manner of propagation is supposed to be by a sort of tremor or undulation. The motion of a wave over the surface of water partially illustrates this view. The ripple caused by casting a stone into water, in the celerity, uniformity, and rapidity with which it spreads in every direction,

is a very striking expression of the wave theory of light. Equally to the point, is the conveyance of sound through the atmosphere. In this we do not so readily perceive the action, but we can often hear it in the reverberations caused by projecting points, and in the vibrations sound itself, caused in passing over a tight string, as a fiddle string, or any frail elastic substance, as a thin tube of glass, a drum-head, a sheet of metal, &c.

Both of these hypotheses appear probable, though they widely differ. Both afford an explanation of many phenomena; but they are both beset by difficulties of a grave character. If, for example, light is made up of particles of ponderable matter, however small these particles may be, would they not, with a motion of 200,000 miles a second, possess, in an eminent, an irresistible degree, the power of impact—one of the most tremendous forces in nature? See what the slight tap of a hammer will do. It will impress and indent bodies to an extent which it would require tons of pressure to produce. Even a tallow candle, projected from a gun at the rate of only 1,000 feet per second, will pass through an inch board. Would not those little things, luminous particles of light, so small indeed that millions of them, collected by a lens, are imperceptible through the strongest microscope—so small that they must be sharper than the finest point of which we have any knowledge—would they not, I say, penetrate everything—not only the tender coats of the eye, but the hardest and most opaque bodies? Would they not, like other projectiles, destroy everything mortal? And would not iron, and brass, and marble, and wood, lose all reflective power, and become as transparent as glass. With objections to the atomic theory thus weighty, must we not infer that light is something far different from ponderable matter?

If so, are we to settle down upon the ethereal view? By so doing, we will have to encounter another class of objections, arising from the fact itself of imponderability. Is it possible that there exists a fluid, or gas, so inconceivably thin as to pass through the gaseous elements, the liquids, &c., and in so few instances have its properties altered? If light is a fluid, or gas, is it not possessed of chemical properties? and if so, how can it mingle so freely with so many chemical agents, and, as it were, "run the gauntlet" untouched and uninjured? These and many other objections to both of these views, are of a grave character. Still, I do not say they are unanswerable. The whole subject of the nature of light, not only in my mind, but in the minds of the most profound philosophers, is involved in much obscurity. The properties of light are better understood.

One property of light is that it is propagated from luminous bodies in all directions. This is true not only of the sun's light, but of the electric spark, phosphorescence, a red hot iron, or the flame of a candle. The sun illumines, not only the earth, but the planets, comets, and all bodies in the firmament. A simple demonstration of this proposition, is by placing a lamp, or candle, in the centre of a room, and observing it from different points.

A second property of light is, that in a homogeneous medium, it always moves in straight lines. Light will not travel through a bent tube, but it passes freely through a straight tube. Again, if three cards, or plates of metal, each pierced with a small hole, are placed in such a position as that the holes are exactly opposite to each other, the light will pass freely through them, but if the holes are not in a straight line the light will not pass.

A third property of light is, that it requires time for its propagation. Within any terrestrial distance its passage may be regarded as instantaneous. Astronomy furnishes the means, not only of detecting its actual propagation, but of measuring its velocity with great precision. The eclipses and emersions of Jupiter's satellites become visible about 16 minutes 26 seconds earlier when the earth is at its least distance from Jupiter, than when it is at its greatest. It requires, therefore, about fifteen minutes for light to travel through the earth's orbit. Now, the sun's distance from the earth being about 95,000,000 of miles, it follows that light travels with the prodigious velocity of nearly

200,000 miles in a second. At this rate it would encircle the earth in the eighth part of a second. This calculation appears incredible, but no result of science is more certain.

Another property of light is reflection. When it falls on a smooth polished surface, it does not stay there, and is not absorbed as when it encounters other bodies, such as black velvet, but it is returned from the surface at an angle equal to the angle of incidence, and continues the new direction in a straight line, as before the reflection. The quantity of light thus reflected depends on the nature and polish of the surface, and on the angle of incidence, being greatest when that angle is small. None of the ordinary reflectors, as tin, silver plate, mercury, speculum-metal, &c., reflect more than three-fourths of the incident light. But a properly constructed reflector, made of the best French plate-glass, and silvered by my silvering process,* reflects nearly all the light. A piece of one of my mirrors, placed at an angle in front of a camera lens, will give a picture almost, if not quite as quickly as the lenses alone. I have a plan, recently devised, by which I can form a reflector for the telescope of any required dimensions—say within twelve feet diameter. It will be made on glass, and yet have no one objection arising from the inequalities of structure which exist in all glass. The plan consists in silvering a large and very perfect glass, backing up the silver by a novel, but easy method, and then detaching it from the glass. The objection of " double reflection," one from the silver, and one from the surface of the glass, and of distortion, occasioned by the inequalities of the glass, would be completely obviated. At the same time, the reflector would be far more level than metal can be made in any other way, and the polish is an incomparable distance ahead of what can be obtained in any other way.

A fifth property of light is refraction; that is, its susceptibility of being bent or turned from its course on its entering

* Now owned, and most successfully worked, by the "American Glass Silvering Company," New York.

certain media. The angle of refraction depends on the nature of the medium. In the liquids, and most of the uncrystallized substances, the refraction is all in one direction. In most crystallized media, part of the refracted light follows one course, and part of it a different one. In this case the refraction is said to be double.

The last property of light which I shall mention here, is its relations to actinism and heat. It was long thought that the chemical changes induced through the agency of light are owing to its heat, and it is still a commonly received opinion that these changes are wrought by luminosity. With Sir Robert Hunt, Sir John Herschel, Edmund Becquerel, and other philosophers, I think that it is demonstrable that both of these views are incorrect. Neither heat nor luminosity has much, if anything, to do with these changes. A photograph is the result of the actinic power or property residing in light. A few simple experiments will determine the truth of this view, thus :

1. In each of the seven colors of the spectrum place a thermometer. The one in the red ray will indicate the greatest heat, and so on up to the violet ray, where the heat will be least.

2. Remove the thermometers, and place in the spectrum a sensitive surface, as chloride of silver paper, and you will find that the violet ray, which produced the least heat, will induce the greatest darkening of the paper.

3. Place in the spectrum a strip of white paper, and you will find it most illuminated under the yellow ray—one of the rays which produced so little darkening of the paper. Under the violet ray, where the actinic effect was greatest, the illumination will be very slight.

The same effects may be produced, though not so perfectly, with seven colored glasses, or with bottles filled with colored liquids. In this case the colored media should interpose between the thermometers, the photographic paper, and the plain paper, and the direct rays of the sun.

The lack of photogenic power in the illuminating rays, and the superiority of the non-illuminating rays, as the blue and violet, may also be shown as follows: Prepare a piece of photographic paper, and over one part of it place a yellow glass, and over the other part of it a blue or violet glass, and expose them to the sun equal lengths of time—say three or four minutes. The portion under the yellow glass will be but slightly darkened, while that under the blue, or violet, will be nearly or quite black. A similar difference will be observed in the use of the Daguerreotype plate.

These simple experiments will amply demonstrate the proposition, that the powers of light are distinct from and independent of each other. At the same time they act in perfect harmony, though most intimately blended and compounded together. What I have written above is true of Daguerreotype, Calotype, Ambrotype, Chromatype, Cyanotype, Chrysotype, Energialtype, and the whole category of types in which only light and shade are concerned. I now have to repeat a statement, the first publication of which, about six years ago, in my announcement of the discovery of natural colors, created much surprise, and not a little incredulity in the minds of scientific men. It is this: That the whole philosophy of types, as represented above, in regard to Actinism, or Ray Power, is found to be inapplicable to my Heliochromic processes, excepting, indeed, the relations of heat. In all the results I have attained in natural colors, whether on plates, paper, or collodion, I have found the yellow ray most powerful, the orange next, the light green next, the red next, the indigo next, the blue next, and the violet least. I have also been tormented with the anomaly of the dark green sometimes acting slowly, and frequently not at all, while at other times it works with great energy.

I merely state facts, without feeling any obligation to account for them. Indeed, I can give but one solution of the problem, which is, that mine is a colorific, while the other types are reducing processes. These all reduce the sensitive agents employed to certain conditions of oxide, or to the metallic state, while the heliochrome leaves its surfaces at a great remove from the metallic state, and brings about certain forms of matter productive of color.

It would be interesting to continue this essay on the nature and properties of light; but I have so much to write about which is more immediately connected with the main subject of this volume, that I will forbear. Thus far, I have given no more than a cursory glance at the principal rudiments which lie at the foundation of my grand theme. The next chapter will embrace my views of light as a composition of colored rays, and as the source of all color.

CHAPTER II.

Chromatics—Light a compound of Colored Rays—Proof by the Prism—Iridescence—Coloring Matter and the Chromatic Rays—Porosity of Matter—Curious Properties of Various Bodies—Mica—Mother of Pearl—Iodide of Mercury—The Soap Bubble—Coating of the Daguerreotype Plate—Iodine Rings—Metallo-Chromes—Potatoe growing above Ground—Plants grown in Darkness—Autumnal Leaves—Varnish on Water—Chlorophyle—These instances partly Mechanical and Chemical—Can a Surface be prepared on which Light itself will produce similar Changes?

What is light in respect to its ingredients? What is the character of its component parts? To the eye it appears white. A skilful colorist, with the primary colors on his palette, will compound a tolerable white. The All-wise One, with a few primary colored rays, illuminates our eyes with a pure, soft, perfect white light. Presently I will come to the proof of this fact. For the present I will dwell on the fact itself. Look at a candle blaze. It is white, barring a slight tinge of yellow. The latter is referable to impurities in the tallow. The same is true of oil. Spermaceti is a purer hydro-carbon—so is camphene, or "burning-fluid"—hence their more brilliant light. Olefiant gas is freed from many of its impurities in the manufacture—hence the greater purity of its light. The "Argand Lamp," by giving the blaze an abundance of oxygen, and thus consuming the excess of carbon, affords a very white light. The "Drummond light," by the intense heat of the oxy-hydrogen blaze, strongly ignites a small globe of lime, and gives a light of surprising intensity and clearness. The "Voltaic light" is another instance of the triumph of heat over the impurities which dim the "Holy Thing" called light. But all these instances are but glow-worms compared with that great source of light, the Sun. The emanations from that luminary are perfectly white. True, we never fully see this to be the case—but this is owing to our looking at it, as it were, "through a glass, darkly." That glass is our atmosphere, and the regions of ether beyond. But when we consider that between us and old Sol lies a stratum of air and ether, ninety-six million miles thick, and that the dimness and discoloration occasioned thereby is very slight, may we not say with an inspired writer, "Great and marvellous are thy works, Lord God Almighty."

It is well that the whiteness of light is not perfectly apparent. It would be too much of a stimulus to the visual organs, and would become tedious from its own monotony. As it is, both of these objections are obviated. Not only is the eye constantly bathing in a healthy element, but there is an amazing variety in the softening tints—just enough to give a pleasing diversity, and seldom extending to extremes of contrast. This beautiful arrangement is of the first importance to Photography. If this variation in the whiteness of light was as great as we can imagine it might be—if it was as marked as the changes in the weather, the difficulty of "timing" Camera pictures would be increased to almost an impossibility.

It is now conceded by all respectable opticians, that this colorless white light incloses in its gossamer folds, and may be made to disclose, the most gorgeous and magnificent colors. A simple proof of this is by means of the prism. This contrivance enables us to decompose and examine—than which there is no surer road to certain knowledge. If you pass a ray of sun-light through a piece of flat glass, it will give a white dot on a dark screen. Now, take a triangular glass—in other words, a glass rod ground to three sides, and polished. This is a prism. An icicle, of the same shape, is a prism—so is a three square phial filled with water. The pendants of a parlor lamp, or girandole, though not perfectly triangular, answer very well for prisms. They may be called prismoids. Pass a ray of sun-light through one of these prisms, and you will find on the screen beautiful bands of colors. These colors are seven in number—namely, red, orange, yellow, green, blue, indigo, and violet; and they melt into each other by insensible gradations. It seems impossible to define the limits at which one color ends and another begins. Nothing could be more beautiful than these colors. This is called the solar spectrum. It is a rainbow, in another shape, and of a reduced size; but the colors of a well defined spectrum are far more brilliant than those of the rainbow. I have said that the spectrum is composed of seven colors. Three of these, red, blue, and yellow, may be regarded as primaries; the other four, I believe, are secondary colors, compounded from the primaries. Blue and yellow form green; red and blue form violet; red and yellow form orange; and as for the indigo ray, I think it is blue, intermingled with some of the dark lines of the spectrum, of which there are about 600, or with violet.

There are many other instances of the prismatic decomposition of white light. The colors on mother of pearl, mica, and other striated and grooved surfaces, are referable to this cause, though the modus of the phenomenon is very difficult to explain. The iridescence, or play of colors, produced by thin films of matter, is another result of the same law. Sprinkle a little spirit varnish on the surface of water, and you will have the effect perfectly. You may even lift out the delicate interminglings on a sheet of paper, and they will remain permanent. They cannot fade unless the material which forms the film is photogenic, for the color depends on the form and relative degrees of tenuity of the matter.

We now arrive at a most vital part of our theory. What is coloring matter? or, what is colored matter? or, is there any such thing as colored matter? That is, is there a specific coloring principle in matter, irrespective of the colored rays of light? I hold that there is not. Practical Heliochromy teaches me, at every step, that all color is due to light; the nature of the color of any piece of matter is governed by the form of that matter;

and the way the form of bodies governs their colors is on the principle of absorption and refraction. What I mean is this : a given body, for example gold, will absorb all the colors but one ; that one colored ray (in the case of gold it is yellow) will remain unabsorbed on the surface, and be refracted to the eye as a certain color, and strike the senses as if the body was colored specifically by some inherent coloring principle. All bodies are porous, In other words, matter is filled with holes. These holes, or pores, vary in size and shape. The ultimate particles of light, also, we may suppose, vary in size and shape. Of course a given form of matter will absorb certain rays, and retain on its surface, and refract other rays. A piece of carmine will absorb all the rays but the red; indigo all but the blue ; chrome yellow all but the yellow. This, these substances will do even in thin strata. Other substances will retain on their surfaces two of the primaries at once—hence the formation of green, violet, orange, and their innumerable tints. Change the form of the matter, and the color changes at once without the intervention of any specific coloring principle. Even gold in a certain form is a dark mahogany brown, instead of yellow. This is the case where gold is precipitated from its solution by sulphate of iron. Gold in this form is very pure. Melt the dark powder in a crucible, and presto, change, you again have the yellow metal. Some bodies change with great facility, and with every change of form is a different color. Take for an example, the soap-bubble. As it enlarges or contracts you will observe a constant change of colors. The coating of a Daguerreotype plate with the vapor of iodine is another case to the point. The iodine is grey—its vapor is violet—but as the coating progresses you have yellow, orange, red, blue, green. In thickening the film of iodide of silver you constantly change the form or structure of this compound, and as constantly have a change of color. Expose this plate to light for a prolonged period, and it will again pass through a series of beautiful colors. Expose it a very short time to light and it acquires an affinity for mercurial vapor. The amalgam formed by this vapor is white. All colorific effects, with an occasional exception, are destroyed by this process. The exceptions referred to are quite remarkable. The Illuminated Daguerreotype, invented and patented by Mr. Ilsley, of New York, is a striking illustration of my theory. The plate, after exposure in the camera, is placed over a mat opening, at the distance of the thirty-second part of an inch, and mercurialized. The mercury in creeping around the edge of the mat produces rings of rainbow colors. The mercury, doubtless, goes on irregularly, producing a striated surface, similar to that of mother of pearl, and hence the colors. Daguerreotypists have occasionally been amazed by the formation of some one color on their plates. Mr. Becker, of New York, obtained a good brick red in a street view, which he took one day on a waste plate. He sent the result to Voightlaender, of Germany. Mr. Becker tried repeatedly to get a similar effect, but utterly failed. About three years ago Mr. Bodo England, of Philadelphia, then working in my brother's room in Kingston, Yew York, obtained the distant Catskills in good blue, and the fields of the foreground in faint green. This he did on several plates, but afterwards completely failed. I saw the results, and at once referred them to some freak in the refractive action of the light, aided by some peculiarity in the coating of the plate. He told me that his coating had an excess of bromine, and from the appearance of the pictures I am sure the plates had on them a thin layer of organic matter.

Now, before proceeding to other illustrations of this subject, let us reason for a moment on what I have written. Here are facts in regard to the Daguerreotype plate, with which every operator is familiar. How are we to account for them? Certainly not on the principle of specific coloring matter. The color of the iodine vapor, with which this succession of beautiful tints is produced, is violet—only violet. Hence it could not produce anything more than its own color if we regard it as a pigment. The color of mercurial vapor is white; and, as a pigment, would give only white. The color of the brick-house in Mr. Becker's street view, and the hues of the mountains and fields in Mr. England's results, were favorable to the pigmentary view; but how, on this principle, did they ever get to the plate unless we suppose that the actual coloring matter left the brick-house, and travelled into Becker's window, and that the blue of the Catskills, and the green of the Kingston meadows, journeyed through the air, and through the lenses of England's camera, and painted themselves on the plates. Absurd as these suppositions appear, they afford the only explanation of these phenomena aside from the theory I have here advanced.

I will not omit to mention here the Metallo-chromes as an illustration of the same law. In a shallow dish, place a saturated solution of acetate of lead. In the bottom of it place a polished steel plate, connected with the terminating wire of the positive pole of a pair of Grove's batteries; then bring the point of the negative wire into contact with the solution of lead, and there will be produced on the steel-plate a series of colored rings of the most gorgeous beauty. Let the wire terminate with a level plate, cut into figures, and you will have a corresponding effect on the steel. To account for this curious effect, we may suppose that thin, but unequal layers of metallic lead are deposited, and that these are oxydized. The colors and their fine blendings, depend upon the law of absorption and refraction, as in the other cases cited. Another elegant form of the Metallo-chrome may be produced thus: On a polished silver plate place a small crystal of iodine, and gently heat the plate. A series of colored rings are at once formed. They are very beautiful, and depend upon the unequal thickness, or rather unequal thinness, of the circular coatings formed. This experiment is easily tried. Let any intelligent person who may make the trial, as he gazes upon the charming result—the miniature rainbow—pause and inquire, how were these colors formed? and I wager that his conclusions will be—they resulted from the production of certain forms of matter, and from the property acquired by the matter of absorbing some of the colored rays and refracting others. To make the matter still plainer, we will suppose this series of rings to be a sieve. One circle of meshes may be supposed to be of one degree of fineness, the next of another, and so on through the series. Suppose we place in this sieve several colored powders of different degrees of fineness, and of certain relative shapes. Evidently each powder, on shaking the sieve, will be retained in its appropriate circle, and bands of color will be the result. So with the rings of coating formed on the silver plate. One circle has a degree and character of porosity which will absorb, or sift through, all the colored rays save one, or more, and the result is, that that colored ray or rays will be retained on the surface of that ring, and hence the color. So with the whole series. The ocular, though not the chemical property of one ring, will be the same as that of carmine, of another the same as indigo, of another the same as chromate of lead, while others will be, in different degrees, of the same ocular character as the compound pigments or dye-stuffs.

Many of the metallic salts afford very striking illustrations of our theme. We might select almost at random. Say we take iodide of mercury. Its crystals are sometimes red, sometimes yellow. The red may be changed to yellow, and the yellow to red, by the simple contact of a sharp point. The change in the form of the matter is by molecular movement. The red crystals are quadratic, the yellow right rhombic. Change the quadratic to the right rhombic and it becomes yellow, and vice versa. The salts of chrome, manganese, copper, nickel, cobalt, iridium, &c., are equally remarkable for the number and beauty of their colors. In a state of combustion, many of these salts present very curious colorific properties. Chloride of copper burns with a fine green blaze; strontid, red baryta, yellow chromium green; boron, zinc, &c., all burn with a characteristic color.

The vegetable world is equally fruitful in proofs of the theory here advanced. It is well known that plants grown in the dark are colorless. A bulbous root, grown partly in the light and partly in the dark, will be half colored and half colorless. Observing a potato, growing partly out of ground, the portion above ground being green, was one of the first lessons nature taught me in Heliochromy. I reason thus:—the effect could not be due to oxygen, for the portion under ground was so near the surface that it had free access to the oxygen of the air—it could not be owing to the heat of the sun, for I have seen the phenomenon in a shaded place—it is, therefore, the effect of light.

Chlorophyl affords another striking proof of the theory which lies at the foundation of Heliochromy. This singular substance forms the green coloring matter of leaves, grass, &c. "It may be obtained," says Booth, "by treating grass with boiling water, then with alcohol or ether, evaporating or mixing with water, and distilling. It is a green, waxy substance, but we know not whether it be a fat, resin, &c. Its color appears to be easily changed to a yellow." This is all I could ever learn from the books in respect to chlorophyl, excepting a remark of Berzelius, that in the seared leaves of autumn the chlorophyl is displaced by a yellow coloring matter, which he calls Xanthophyl. But I have experimented largely with chlorophyl, of which a full account will be found in the subsequent pages. These experiments will be found very interesting, and afford strong evidence of the correctness of our theory. In this place I will merely dwell briefly on the curious workings of this substance in the great laboratory of nature. Who has not observed and admired the first inception of the green tint in the tender leaf of spring, its gradual increase to a decided green, and the truly grand and magnificent intermingling of red, scarlet, brown russet, crimson, orange, yellow, and remains of green, which these leaves present in that sober season, the autumnal time? No portion of nature's works are more full of beauty, brightness, and divinity. With truth has it been said, that "God dwells not only in the Palace he made for angels, but in every blade of grass, and in every leaf that trembles in the breeze." Poets of the highest order have attuned their songs to the "sweet spring time," when the "tender buds" appear, and nature weaves for herself a robe of green, and no less sweetly and pathetically have they sung the mellow cadence of brown October and rueful November. Well, all this is pretty—it is delicious—it is even enravishing;—but there is a "land of Beulah," to use Bunyan's phrase, back of all this. In the heliochromic view there is utility as well as delight. It teaches us to regard these phenomena as a grand system of "natural colors," and points the way to scientific investigation, and to the possibility of a practical dive into this grand arcanum of nature. So, at least, it taught me, in my first attentions to this subject. I observed that the young leaf is but slightly green. As it thickens and solidifies, its green tint increases; for the reason, doubtless, that it thereby acquires a greater amount, and more perfectly concentrates this quantity of chlorophyl, and therefore more perfectly obstructs the passage of the green rays. At a certain age, and especially under the influence of frost, the coloring matter undergoes a change, and, so to speak, is tumbled into great diversities of molecular form, and the foliage takes on the variegated hues we so much admire. Then the colored rays, as it were, hold a general convocation, and dance a jubilee of a few weeks on the mountain sides, and through the lowly vales, till Jack Frost gives the foliage another and more bitter nip, and the forest is disorganized in a night.

The instances above cited, in which matter assumes forms productive of the absorption and refraction of the colored rays, are partly due to chemical and mechanical causes. Can a surface be prepared on which light itself will produce similar changes? I will reserve the discussion of this question to the next chapter.

The foregoing views are my own—not a mere compilation from authors. Years ago I read Newton, La Place, Euler, Brewster. But as soon as I turned my thoughts to the natural colors, I found it necessary to renounce the controlling influence of other men's theories, and to follow the bent of my own mind, and the suggestions of nature at every step. From that day to this I have thought, and studied, and toiled, in a way of my own. Now that I am preparing my views for the public, my great anxiety is, that they may be tested, and not rejected by any because they do not agree with their theories. Our own mere philosophizings, and those of the wisest savants, are frequently skittish things, and kick hard against practice and facts.

CHAPTER III.

Heliochrome possible—Opinions of Philosophers—Biot, Daguerre, Nicephore Niepce, Sir John Herschel, Sir Robert Hunt—Vulgar Opinions—Argument *à priori*—Chemical Compounds, Decomposition, and Reduction caused or assisted by light.

"DOCTORS differ" on the question "Is Heliochrome possible?" And this difference in the theorizings of philosophers has ever been an antecedent of great discoveries. The discoverer of printing was considered a witch and a devil; Copernicus, who established the doctrine of the earth's motion, was bitterly opposed by the whole religious world; the spinsters and weavers were down upon Arkwright and Whitney; our own Fulton, the inventor of steamboats, was the butt of ridicule in legislative halls, courts, bar-rooms, and other places where blackguards and rowdies form a part of the company; and Professor Samuel F. B. Morse, now immortal, as the inventor of the Magnetic Telegraph, was once a beggar at the doors of Congress; Daguerre, for believing in the possibility of fixing the images of the camera, was regarded by the public as a fool and a humbug. Even his own wife inquired of an eminent philosopher if he thought her husband could be a sane man. All these things seemed impossible. That the same feeling should exist in regard to the natural colors is not surprising.

The learned Biot uses the following language:—"Substances of the same tint may present, in the quantity or the nature of the radiations which they reflect, as many diversities, or diversities of the same order, as substances of a different tint; inversely, they may be similar in their property of reflecting chemical radiations when they are dissimilar to the eye; so that the difference of tint which they present to the eye may entirely disappear in the chemical picture. These are the difficulties inherent in the formation of photographic pictures, and they show, I think, evidently, the illusion of the experimenters who hope to reconcile, not only the intensity, but the tints of the chemical impressions, produced by radiation with the colors of the objects from which these rays emanate." Sir John Herschel, as long ago as 1840, speaking of some faint tintings of color he procured on paper, says:—"I am not prepared to say that this will prove an available process for colored photographs, though it brings the hope nearer." "Here," says Sir Robert Hunt, "we have the speculations of one philosopher representing the production of such pictures as hopeless, while the experiments of another prove them to be within the range of probabilities."

Daguerre, himself, has said that frequently, when he has been copying any red, brick, or painted building, the photograph has assumed a tint of that character; and he labored considerably for the attainment of the colors. So did Nicephore Niepce, his partner, labor to the same end with his bitumen-coated tablets; and the report, though false, went all over Europe that he had actually made the grand discovery. Sir Robert Hunt, already referred to, has advanced quite a lengthy argument on "the possibility of producing photographs in their natural colors." He boldly takes the affirmative, and supports it in his usually able manner. In concluding, he says, "These facts will, I think, prove that the possibility of our being enabled to produce colored photographs is decided, and the probability of it is brought infinitely nearer." M. Edmund Becquerel, one of the profoundest philosophers of Europe, is another advocate of this doctrine.

But as I am not going to fill this chapter with mere opinions, I will come directly to some of the chemical changes wrought by light, especially those resulting in the formation of color. I will start with the flowers of the Cichorium intibus; they are white, or blue, according to the intensity of the day-light. This is a well established fact, and I may justly claim it in support of my theory. Of a similar character is the fact that the rosy and colored aspect of many kinds of fruit is on the side towards the sun. We see this in the apple, peach, strawberry, several varieties of cherry, pear, apricot, &c.

In the animal creation, the influence of light in producing color is equally evident. The tints of polar and subterranean animals are dull and dingy, while those in the tropical regions are bright and gaudy. As a general thing, too, the colored parts of animals are those most exposed to light. Even serpents are no exception to this law; the beautiful colors displayed by many of them being mostly on their backs. The plumage of many of the tropical birds is magnificent. The birds and fowl of northern climates are robed in a more sober guise. Our fine birds, as the yellow bird, the robin, the pigeon, the goose, duck, &c., will bear no comparison with the fine birds of the sunny South, as the ostrich, the flamingo, the ibis, &c. Our peacocks, roosters, &c., are no exception, for they gain their plumes by inheritance from a foreign ancestry, and will not compare with their brethren in the bright regions of the South.

These instances, in connexion with the vast resources of chemistry, would seem sufficient to establish the probability, at least, that art can prepare a surface on which light itself will produce the molecular forms, or modifications of matter essential to the phenomena of color. Let us, however, advert to some of the operations of the laboratory. Take, for example, the art of calico-printing. The bulk of all these colored fabrics fade; that is to say, they are photogenic—yea, verily, they are Heliochromic; for as they pass to the colorless state they go through a great diversity of tints. What is orange now will soon be yellow; the yellow will soon descend to a straw color; the red runs down to pink, and even to various dingy tints of brown and russet; the deep blue degenerates to a mere azure blush; the bright emerald green fades away to a pea-green, &c. &c. All this comes to pass in and out door, in a dry or humid atmosphere, and is plainly the effect of light. In fact the whole operation is a sort of Heliochrome in an inverted order.

The same may be said of oil and water-color paintings. They fade, slowly, it is true; but in fading they pass through the descending chromatic scale. But few colors are permanent, as the term is. The works of a few of the old masters of painting which have retained their brilliancy for hundreds of years, are the astonishment and envy of modern art. It would be just as proper to say that most colors are Heliochromic. Such a remark is as far from being visionary as that of Sir John Herschel, namely, that " nearly all the substances in nature are photogenic."

But it is the chemist, more than all others, who has occasion to observe these remarkable effects of light. Many of his compounds must be kept excluded from light, or both their properties and color will change. Others require light for their perfect formation—while a third class are so sensitive to light at the moment of, or during the process of formation, that they are much more perfectly formed in some countries than others. The best French process for making carmine, for example, could not be successfully worked under the foggy skies of England; and it is probably owing, in a great degree, to the same cause that the Chinese and French vermillion is superior to that made in other countries. Many of the salts of silver may be named as an example of the other class of compounds alluded to. The chloride of silver, for example, is soon changed to a sub-chloride if exposed to light. In the process of changing it passes through several tints of color. Gallo-nitrate of silver is very rapidly decomposed by light, and turns a dark brown by a few minutes exposure: aceto-nitrate of silver is similarly, though not so quickly affected. Iodide of starch cannot be formed pure in the light, but on the instant of its formation passes to a dark sub-iodide. In these and many similar changes we have a great variety of colors. In some cases the compound is influenced only by a certain class of rays. Herschel noticed that lime-water added to solution of chloride of platinum only afforded a precipitate in white or violet, and not in yellow or red light. Etherial solution of perchloride of iron is changed into proto-chloride, behind white and blue, but not red glass. Etherial solution of corrosive sublimate affords calomel under the influence of white and blue, but not of red light. Solution of peroxalate of iron is decomposed by white, violet, and blue light, into carbonic acid and protoxalate; but red light fails of this effect. Iodide of starch, which is blue, is bleached under white, green, and yellow light; red and blue light affect it but little; violet not at all. Chloride of silver, by a prolonged exposure to the red ray, is slightly tinted with the natural color of the ray; under yellow, orange, and green, it is eventually darkened, though slowly; under the blue and violet it is rapidly changed to a blue, purple, sepia, black, and at last, to a bronze-like, coppery green.

In the illustration drawn from calico-printing, it will be noticed that the colors which occur in the fading process were on the descending chromatic scale. In many of the above instances the reverse is true. The formation of color begins with the faintest tint, and ascends to the maximum of colorific effect. The former is not, therefore, so perfect as a heliochromic phenomenon as the latter; but it will scarcely be denied by any logician, that from these two classes of phenomenon we have constructed a good *à priori* argument in support of the possibility of heliochromy. Much more might be written under this head, but it would be foreign to my purpose to even mention, in tabular form, the vast number of facts similar to the above, which the science of chemistry affords. Besides, I will not anticipate what will more appropriately come under the head of "EXPERIMENTS."

CHAPTER IV.

Antiquity—The Jugglers of Ancient India—The Alchemists—Chloride of Silver—Scheele—M. Berard—Seebeck—Berthollet—Sir William Herschel—Wollaston's Experiments on Gum Guiacum—Sir Humphrey Davy—Oxyde of Lead—The Action of the Colored Rays—Wedgewood and Davy's First Pictures—Daguerre and Niepce's First Experiments—Their Copartnership—The Bitumen Process—Discovery of the Daguerreotype—Action of the French Government—Talbot and his Process—The First Portrait from Life—Prof. Morse—Daguerre, Niepce, Talbot, Sir John Herschel, and Sir Robert Hunt, work for the Colors—Iridescence—Complementary Colors—Becquerel—Niepce de St. Victor—My claim to Priority fully Examined—The United States Senate—My Early Pictures—The "Infernal Committee"—Certificates.

"The progress of discovery is ordinarily a slow process, and it often happens that a great fact is allowed to lie dormant for years or for ages, which, when eventually revived, is found to render a fine interpretation of some of Nature's harmonious phenomena, and to minister to the wants or pleasures of existence."—Robert Hunt. *Treat. on Photography, p.* 1.

It would seem essential to the proper elucidation of this part of my subject, that I should give at least a running outline of the history of Photography in the common acceptation of that term, as embracing the whole family of light and shade pictures.

If we go back to antiquity we shall find but little to write about. Although the artisans of olden times had a very perfect knowledge of some beautiful processes, we have no evidence that they knew anything whatever of practical photography. The statement that the Jugglers of Ancient India could "copy the profile of any individual by the action of light," appears to be of a piece with many other extravagant assertions of their skill. At least they are ignorant of any such process at present.

The Alchemists, in searching, by a great multiplicity of manipulations, for the philosopher's stone and the elixir vitæ, hit upon horn silver, as they called the fused chloride of silver, and observed and recorded the fact, that it was blackened by light. They did not even think, as far as we can learn, of applying the fact to photographic use; but stupidly used it as an argument to prove the doctrine that "silver only differed from gold in being mercury interpenetrated by the sulphurous principle of the sun's rays." We should give them credit, however, for leaving a record of the blackening.

To that profound scholar and philosopher, Scheele, are we indebted for the first scientific examination of this remarkable phenomenon. His experiments resulted in proving the "dissimilar powers of the different rays of light in effecting this change." In the year 1801, Ritter demonstrated that rays existed beyond the visible spectrum, which had the property of "speedily blackening chloride of silver." These researches commanded the attention of such men as M. Bérard, Seebeck, Berthollet, Sir William Herschell, Sir Henry Englefield. Their investigations led to much information in regard to the luminous, heating, and chemical powers of the colored rays. Dr. Wollaston pursued and published some most interesting experiments on the effects of light on gum guaiacum. He found that "paper washed with a solution of this gum in spirits of wine, had its yellow color rapidly changed to green by the violet rays, while the red rays had the property of restoring the yellow hue." Sir Humphrey Davy observed that the puce-colored oxyde of lead was reddened under the red ray, and blackened under the violet ray; that hydrogen and chlorine entered into combination more rapidly in the red than in the violet rays, and that the green oxyde of mercury, although not changed by the most refrangible rays, speedily became red in the least refrangible.

None of these discoveries were applied to picture making, though we look back upon them with pleasure, as they laid the foundation for the splendid superstructure which has since been reared. The first attempts at fixing images by light were published in the Journal of the Royal Institution of Great Britain, in June, 1802. These were by those eminent philosophers, Wedgewood and Davy. The former, as far back as the year 1800, devised the following " pretty experiment." He stretched a piece of paper, or other convenient material, upon a frame, and sponged it over with a solution of nitrate of silver; he then placed it behind a painting on glass, and exposed the arrangement to light. A " kind of copy of it" was produced upon the prepared paper. This experiment may be regarded as the origin of the art of photography. From the fact of Wedgewood employing a painting instead of a print, I feel almost authorized to set him down as the man who first attempted to discover heliochromy.

Neither Wedgewood nor Davy succeeded in rendering their preparations sufficiently sensitive for the camera. By means of the solar microscope the latter procured a faint image; but he could not fix or fasten the impression, and the grand theme was abandoned in despair.

In 1814, M. Niepce and M. Daguerre took up the subject. In 1829 they entered into co-partnership. In 1827 M. Niepce presented specimens of his heliographs, as he called them, and a statement to the Royal Society of London, but they were rejected (most illiberally, I think), on the ground that he did not give his process. This, as it has since appeared, consisted in coating a tablet of glass, silver, or tin, with resin or asphaltum, dissolved in essential oil, as lavender, or in alcohol, exposing to the luminous influence for one or more days, and washing away the parts unacted upon by light, with the solvent. Paper impregnated with the nitrate or chloride of silver, was the material first used by Daguerre. His first attempts were scarcely more encouraging than those of Wedgewood. The discovery of the daguerreotype was reported to the world in January, 1839. The process was made known in the following July, after the passage of an act by the French government securing to Daguerre an annuity of 6,000 francs, and to M. Isidore Niepce, the son of Daguerre's partner, an annuity of 4,000 francs, with one half in reversion for their widows.

In January, 1839, six months previous to the publication of Daguerre's process, Mr. Fox Talbot, an Englishman, made known to the Royal Society his discovery, and the next month published his process on paper—the Talbot-type. Mr. Talbot secured himself by patent, for which he has been most bitterly and unjustly censured. From his process has grown the beautiful paper Photography, as now practised, and the still more beautiful process for Positives on glass. I am not alone in the rapidly growing opinion, that Talbot's laurels will yet be brighter than Daguerre's.

From the periods referred to the progress of Photography has been rapid. At first the Daguerreotype was used only for still objects, as landscapes, architecture, &c.; but it was not long before the ever-progressive Yankees applied it to portraits from life. Had it remained in the hands of Daguerre, he might never have improved it so far. Inventors seldom perfect their own processes.

I have taken much pains to ascertain who was the first person who took a Daguerreotype from life. Dr. Draper, and Professors Wolcott and Morse, were among the first who attempted the achievement in the city of New York. Prof. Morse's first attempt was on the roof of a house in Broadway. The subject was his own daughter. She sat heroically for twenty minutes in brilliant sunshine, with her eyes closed, of course. Success crowned the effort in the development of a very fair picture. I will not say that this was the first portrait from life by the Daguerreotype, but I am strongly inclined to think it was. Prof. Morse, to whom I put the question, was too modest to answer it decidedly.

About half a century has now elapsed since Wedgewood took the first step in Photography. It is forty years since Daguerre, Niepce, and Talbot, commenced their investigations. It is about seventeen years since their discoveries were made public.

About ten years ago the Daguerreotype in a few skilful hands, began to show the maximum of its capabilities. Now, both Daguerreotyping and Talbotyping, and the kindred processes which have grown out of them, have attained a degree of perfection truly surprising.

During all these labors for the discovery and improvement of these arts, it is safe to assert, that a latent wish has been almost universally felt for the attainment of Heliochromy. Indeed, it is quite probable that with most experimenters there has been an ardent longing, a good deal of hoping, and some effort. We have proof that Daguerre considered the object attainable. He theorized much, and sometimes well, on this subject; and he tried many experiments—many, no doubt, for which the world is no wiser. This great man, to whom the world is so much indebted, was a quiet, unassuming gentleman, with large bumps of secretiveness and caution. In his account of his "instantaneous process," as it was called, he exhibits a familiar acquaintance with the laws governing the molecular arrangement of matter, and proves himself an acute reasoner, alive to the whole subject of actinism, or ray power; more so, indeed, than we could expect from the partial mind of an inventor.

Niepce, as we stated in a previous chapter, did not hesitate to let it be known that he was seeking after the colors, and the report went far and near that he had found them. Talbot, as it would appear from many things in his writings, has had the same rosy dreams, and gone through similar efforts in his seekings after this precious gem.

Sir John Herschel, the eminent astronomer and philosopher, has had much of his attention directed this way. Several years ago he actually succeeded in procuring, upon photographic paper, impregnated with the colored juice of flowers, a faint-colored image of the solar spectrum. Afterwards he wrote—"I have got specimens of paper, long kept, which give a considerably better representation of the spectrum in its natural colors than I had obtained at the date of my paper (February, 1840), and that light on a dark ground."

Now, from this, and corroborating testimony, it appears that Herschel did discover a method of producing natural colors in the year of our Lord 1840. Justice requires me to record this as a fact. Neither would I twist my pen to abate the honor which is his due. But the same justice (to myself) requires me to state, that his pictures were on paper, while mine (the early ones) are on silver plates; his required several days for their formation, while mine are often produced in as many seconds; his were very faint, mere tintings, while my pictures are more decided, plain, bold, and brilliant than any other class of sun-drawn pictures. In a word, Herschel himself ignores all claim to an "available process," and only claims for his process that "it brings the hope nearer."

Sir Robert Hunt, a most indefatigable experimenter, a man of science, and very able writer on photography, says in his treatise —"My own experiments have, in many instances, given me colored pictures of the prismatic spectrum, dark upon a light ground; but the most beautiful I have yet obtained has been upon the daguerreotype iodidated tablets, on which the colors have, at the same time, had a peculiar softness and brilliancy." In the Philosophical Magazine for April, 1840, is an able paper from Mr. Hunt, entitled, "Experiments and Observations on Light which has permeated Colored Media." In this he describes some "curious results" on "some of those photographs which are prepared with the hydriodic salts, exposed to luminous influence with colored fluids superimposed." The violet, blue, green, yellow, and red rays produced, not their natural, but their complementary colors. Some pieces of paper which Mr. Hunt prepared with the bi-chromate of potash and a very weak solution of nitrate of soda, were exposed under colored glasses for two dull days in a window having a southern aspect, and gave "tintings" of blue, green, and red.

It will not be claimed either by Mr. Hunt or his friends, that producing "complementary" colors is heliochromy. Nor that the "tintings" on the chromated paper could entitle him to the claim of having discovered the natural colors in the broad meaning of the words. His results on the "iodidated tablets," deserve a few remarks. Such a tablet—in other words, a prepared daguerreotype plate—will give all Mr. Hunt claims; but how, and in how long a time? I answer (for I am familiar with the experiment), that the iodized plate will turn all manner of colors, when exposed to the colored rays, and will, in the course of these changes, assume the colors of the image impinging on it, and that too (not always, however), in their proper localities. In order to secure proof of this effect it is essential to "watch it close," and to stop the action the lucky moment you happen to discover the rose on the right bush. Evidently there is no specific, direct formation of natural colors by this process. I have found from actual and repeated trial, that if, instead of the spectrum, you direct the camera to seven dark bands of different degrees of shading, and these well blended, you will get the same results as those produced by Mr. Hunt; that is, the plate, under the reducing action of the light, as it goes through its transformation or metamorphoses, so to speak, will be so affected by the relative strengths of the light, as to present the phenomenon in question.

In my process there is evidently a specific action of the colored rays, which form, or produce, the natural colors, and no others, either before or after the proper time of exposure to light. Remove one of my plates from the camera before it has had sufficient light to produce a full development of the colors, and where it should be red, blue, or yellow, it will begin to show those colors. Over-expose a plate and the colors are still there, though weakened. This is true, not only of the few primaries, as bright red, blue, and yellow, but with a well prepared plate the same thing holds good with every possible tint and combination of color I have ever attempted to copy. I once counted, by the aid of several practised eyes, the number of tints on 50 of my plates. They amounted to over four hundred.

These remarks are not meant as a disparagement of Mr. Hunt. I am in the most friendly relations with him. About a year ago a friend of mine wrote to Mr. Hunt and Sir John Herschel, giving a carefully drawn up account of the character of my discovery. In reply Mr. Hunt wrote a long and friendly letter, in behalf of himself and Sir John, offering their good offices towards the introduction of the process in Europe, and manifesting the utmost interest in my discovery.

M. Edmund Becquerel, in experiments made in 1849–50, succeeded in producing, on metallic plates, the colors of the spectrum, and copied some colored prints. His process was as follows : Into a jar of muriatic acid, diluted with from 1 to 2 parts of water, he placed a silver plate, having previously connected it with the positive pole of a galvanic battery, the negative pole of which was terminated by a strip of platinum. The silver and platinum plates were kept about one inch apart until the former became coated with the nascent chlorine to a violet hue. It was then rinsed and dried, and exposed to the colored rays. After an exposure of from one to two days a colored image was formed. It was but seldom he obtained more than one or two colors at once. These were usually not brilliant, and were always evanescent. He abandoned the process long since.

During the year 1851, M. Niepce de St. Victor, a nephew of Daguerre's partner, appeared before the world in the usual mystic and swelling style of the French school, as the discoverer of Heliochromy. It was distinctly stated by his organ, *La Lumerie*, that M. Niepce made his announcement at that particular time in consequence of a " publication abroad." This " publication abroad," gentle reader, was no less than the letters of your humble servant, L. L. Hill, which appeared in the *Photographic Journal* and the *Daguerrean Journal*, in which I distinctly claimed to have discovered a process for copying the colors of nature on silver plates. These letters were published several months prior to St. Victor's announcement. Besides, the fact of my having arrived at the discovery was published some four months previous to my letters in the Journals; thus placing me nearly a year ahead of my transatlantic contemporary.

I do not pretend that Niepce made no discovery independently of his knowledge of mine. This I freely concede; also, that his process has enabled him and others to copy colors. I am perfectly willing that he should have all the credit which belongs to him; but I am not willing that he, or his advocates, should rob me of mine. M. Niepce, viewed merely in the light of a claimant, has had many advantages over me in the backing up line. The French savans, than whom there is not a class of intelligent men on earth so much given to fuss and parade and bombast, have backed him. Louis Napoleon has backed him, by giving him an idle office in the "Von Grand Army;" and my enemies in this country (certain Daguerreotypists, I refer to, who hated because they could not govern me), have made the best use they could of this foreigner's Memoirs, to invalidate my claim to this grand discovery, worked out in the Catskill mountains, within the very hearing of the wolf's howl and the panther's screech; and, what is worse, amid poverty and sickness.

This whole matter—my early and later pictures—my chemical coatings—the dates of my announcements—and the dates of all other claims—I, in person, laid before the SENATE OF THE UNITED STATES; and the following is their report. I give it entire, italicizing and capitalizing those portions of which I feel especially proud. It is a document upon which I place higher value than I would upon a laurel crown from the hand of a Cæsar.

From the National Intelligencer.

THE HILLOTYPE.

"The subject of the subjoined report was made on the 3d instant, by one of the committees of the Senate. Being of interest to the general reader, as well as to the scientific class, we insert it in full.

"Mr. JAMES made the following report, which was ordered to be printed:

"The Committee on Patents and the Patent Office, to whom was referred the memorial of Levi L. Hill, in reference to his alleged discovery in Heliochrome, or sun painting, so denominated by said Hill, ask leave to submit the following report:

"Mr. Hill having been before the committee, and explained to them the history and principles of his invention, and submitted to their inspection numerous specimens of the production of his art or invention: the committee have formed the opinion that those specimens afforded *sufficient proofs* that the inventor has *sclved the problem of photographic coloration.* The committee had in their hands the plates, unprotected by glass or any other covering, and saw them freely rubbed and otherwise tested, confirming in their minds the fact of the invention, and the durability of the pictures. It is believed that most of the philosophers, both in Europe and America, long since gave up as hopeless the search after this branch of science, which has been discovered by one of our own citizens, in one of the wild valleys of the Catskill mountains, far removed from the schools of art. The committee learn that Mr. Hill has arrived at this discovery, by which the works of nature may be copied in their original hues, through three years of persevering toil. The committee is informed by Mr. Hill, that his discovery has not as yet been perfected in its practical details, which is not surprising, it being but little more than two years since he obtained his first result. But the *beauty of the results* to which the process has already attained, would seem to afford evidence that it will be perfected at no distant day.

"The prospective utility and importance of this invention, are very important in its application to portraits, landscapes, botany, morbid anatomy, mineralogy, or conchology, aboriginal history, the reproduction of valuable paintings, and to various other ornamental purposes. The committee are satisfied of Mr. Hill's claim to ORIGINALITY and PRIORITY of invention, and deem it just and right that he should be suitably protected and encouraged; and they deem it more particularly so, *seeing that a rival claim has been set up in France since the announcement of his discovery was made.* The means by which this process is carried out being strictly chemical, it would seem that the existing patent laws would not afford to the inventor the security required. Owing, however, to the short period remaining of the present session of Congress, and the press of business, the committee have been unable to devise any better or more efficient mode by which to recognise the claims of Mr. Hill, than by recommending that his memorial, together with this report, be placed on the records of the Senate."

I shall now proceed to give a condensed account of other testimony, by which I hope to satisfy every unprejudiced reader, of the justness of my claim to this grand discovery, and of my PRIORITY in it.

1. In the first place, M. Niepce's discovery was announced several months after mine, and it was made long after I obtained my first results.

2. I was perfectly familiar with the very process he claims, long before he pretends to have made the discovery. Long before his announcement, I exhibited results obtained by chloridating a silver plate, by means of a solution of chloride of copper, mixed with hydro-chloric acid. My first experiments consisted in heating the solution upon a Daguerreotype portrait and view. This gave me several colors all over the pictures, and ended with a fine ruby red, under which the pictures were but slightly obscured. I then coated a naked plate in the same way, and exposed it to light, with a colored engraving superimposed. The result was just such natural colors as those described by Niepce. Like his they very soon began to fade; but unlike those of his which he exhibited in the Crystal Palace in London, they did not fade out; for I put them in a dark place, and they remain to this day. I then continued experimenting until I arrived at a process by which I took a view of my nearest neighbor's house. At that time (which was a year previous to Niepce's publication), the north end of said house had one window less than it had three months before the date of Niepce's announcement. That picture I have shown to a great number of persons, and it demonstrates my priority over Niepce, as the circumstances in respect to the windowless picture could not have existed on any other supposition.

3. I did exhibit specimens in natural colors several months previous to Niepce's claim. This I could easily show by the affidavits of highly respectable persons, if it were necessary. The reason I did not make a public exhibition may be found in my bump of caution. I was afraid it would endanger my secret.

4. As soon as my claim and my truth and veracity were seriously called in question, I began to collect certificates. I was too much engaged in my labors to make a short job of this by going abroad with my pictures. I merely obtained the voluntary statements of some of those who chanced to visit me, excepting in the case of Prof. Morse, whom I sent for during a severe attack of bleeding at the lungs, which led me to fear my life was drawing to a close. Soon after his visit he favored me with the following certificate, which, with many others, was published in the *New York Daily Times* of Oct. 26, 1852.

POUGHKEEPSIE, N. Y., Oct. 6, 1852.

REV. L. L. HILL—MY DEAR SIR:—It gives me great pleasure to testify, from ocular demonstration, to the reality of your discovery of a process for fixing the colors of the camera obscura image. The results you showed me, especially one of a bird of varied plumage, taken in two seconds, showed conclusively that the blues, yellows, and reds were distinctly given and fixed. That there should be imperfections in the manipulation of a new process, and that you should therefore desire to be so familiar with it as to bring it before the public in a perfect form, are circumstances natural and to be expected. But the reality of your discovery is beyond question; you have laid the foundation on which will be built a splendid structure. Every stone, and the finish of each, or of the whole building, it may not be in your power, from your feeble health, to give; but whoever builds must build on your foundation. The astonishing tenacity of the colors upon your plates, yielding neither to rubbing nor ordinary exposure, is a distinct feature of the greatest importance. So also is the quickness of the process, which, when more exactness of manipulation is attained, will enable you to fix at will the more fleeting hues of nature, particularly in the atmospheric tints, and the expressive colors of the complexion of a portrait. The beauty of the flesh tints in the two female heads from nature, which you showed me, and those also in the full length of your little daughter, fully verified this.

M. Becquerel, one of the most indefatigable and illustrious savans of Europe, has had his great mind, with all its garnishments of scientific facts, directed to the solution of the problem fixing the colors of the Camera image, and the result, if report is true, is failure: "he was never able to fasten the colors." M. St. Victor has also obtained results ingenious and beautiful, but I learn that they are equally evanescent. But even if they were permanent, the length of time required to fix the image is fatal for all the varied practical purposes to which yours is applicable. Portraits cannot be taken by a process requiring "two hours," or even "fifteen minutes." Your discovery, so far as I am yet apprised of the labors of scientific men, is unequal, and yet the only one which promises in its perfected state, the great ends desired.

With respect, your friend and servant,

SAMUEL F. B. MORSE.

I also subjoin the following, with the remarks of the New York *Evening Post,* because it forms an essential part of this history, and because it is an outspoken document from a source which every reasonable man will respect. The cutting remark of the professor concerning "some who are not only a disgrace to their profession, but to human nature itself," refers more particularly to the so-called "committee" of the so-called "New York State Daguerrean Association," who after visiting my house, and after my refusal to show them my pictures, reported the whole thing as an "unmitigated delusion." I will add that his words have been verified in the subsequent conduct of the chairman of said "committee," who has been found guilty by a legal tribunal of perjury and arson, and has fled to Europe. Another member of the committee, Mr. Tomlinson, then of Troy, N. Y., has amply atoned to me by letter, for the part he took in this nefarious affair.

From the New York Evening Post, October 19, 1852.

PHOTOGRAPHIC COLORS.

The following communication from Professor Morse, one of the eminent painters of our country, who held for nineteen years the Presidency of the National Academy of the Art of Design, and whose reputation as a man of science is world-wide, appears in the *National Intelligencer*, and will be read with pleasure by all whose love of country is gratified by every new achievement among us in science, skill, and art:

GENTLEMEN—I have just read in a letter of your Paris correspondent some remarks on the subject of "Colored Daguerreotypes," in which allusion is made to Mr. Hill, of Westkill, New York, and in which it is stated that Mr.

Hill has yet exhibited no specimens of his discovery, while "M. Niepce St. Victor, nephew of the celebrated discoverer of photography in France, has made the grand discovery, and showed his pictures to the world." It was also stated, that "M. Becquerel had produced colored pictures, but he was never able to fasten the colors." On this subject, allow me a few remarks in justice to the American discoverer of colored photographs. I received a letter from Mr. Hill a few days since, desiring to see me. He was under the apprehension that he could not live long, having suffered from a violent hemorrhage, which he supposed was from the lungs, and brought on by his untiring devotion to the perfection of his discovery. On the 1st instant I visited him, some sixty miles from this place. I found him so far recovered as to be again able to renew his labors, and, I am happy to say, to induce the belief that the hemorrhage was not from the lungs.

On a previous visit a year since, he showed me no specimens of his discovery; but from the character of the man, and his manner, I believed him to be strictly truthful and honest, and I was satisfied either that he had made the discovery which he had claimed, or was under an honest delusion in respect to it; but I could not then testify to its actuality from personal knowledge. On the evening of the 1st and morning of the 2d instant, however, all doubt of the substantial fact that a great discovery in photography had been made by Mr. Hill was dispelled, by his showing me some twenty specimens of his results. The *most* of them were, like *all* those of M. St. Victor, "*copies of colored engravings.*" They were taken by the camera, and not, as has been reported, "mere transfers of colored prints;" but *all* were not "copies of colored engravings." Two were exquisitely beautiful portrait heads from life, and one a full-length of a child from life. One a landscape view from nature, principally buildings, which, although imperfect in parts, served from that very circumstance to verify to me the genuineness of the discovery. The conclusions to which I came from what I saw are these:

First. Mr. Hill has made the discovery of a process for fixing the colors of the camera image, and, although not so perfected in all its complicated parts as to be equally true in the color in the various objects, is sufficiently developed in its results to give assurance of its ultimate perfection.

Second. Mr. Hill, in delaying hitherto to impart to the public a discovery of such importance, while he has any hope of making it more perfect, has acted with a wisdom and propriety which will be appreciated by the public, and by none more than the most distinguished and honorable of the daguerreotype professors.

Third. None but the most skilful and taste-endowed practitioners of the present photography may expect to succeed in developing the full excellence of Mr. Hill's discovery. It must be in the hands of no ordinary man, but will require for the production of a perfect picture, the taste, the skill, the feeling of thorough and accomplished artists.

Fourth. Mr. Hill's process cannot be like M. Becquerel's, for it is stated that M. Becquerel "was never able to fix the colors," while the colors in Mr. Hill's process are so fixed that the most severe rubbing with a buffer only increases their brilliancy; and no exposure to light has as yet been found to impair their brightness. Nor can it be like M. Niepce St. Victor's; for "fifteen minutes," it seems, is the least time in which some of his results were obtained, while ordinarily, "it takes two hours of exposure" to produce them. Mr. Hill's, on the contrary, are produced in twenty seconds at most, and the most brilliant and most beautiful specimens he showed me were produced in two seconds. I also learn the specimens exhibited by M. Niepce, at the Great Exhibition, were so evanescent, that they perished before the exhibition was closed.

Fifth. I could not but reflect on the different positions of those who are engaged in Europe and America in unfolding this great scientific mystery. The experimenters of Europe have around them, and at command, all the appliances of art, all the compounds, the products of the chemical labors of the world's best scientific minds, ample pecuniary means to pursue their researches; they are further encouraged by the sympathy of the world of art, and national patriotism further rallies to the protection of their country's claims, to the honor of such a discovery.

But how is it with the American experimenter? Shut up in the sequestered valley of the Catskill Mountains, with no appliances of art at his command, and purchasing and transporting at an expense almost ruinous to him the scanty stock of chemicals with which he is to operate; with comparatively few about him to sympathize with him in his labors but a devoted wife, willingly sharing in his privations; with feeble health and limited means, he untiringly pursues his researches at the hazard of all he has in the world, even of life itself, that he may give to the world his perfected discovery. But at least such a man has the sympathy of those to whom his discovery will be of the deepest interest? The professors of the daguerreotype art will hail with delight, and award to the discoverer the highest meed of honor? Americans, too, will feel a pride in sustaining their country's claim to the discovery? What shall I say in answer to these questions? Yes, it is true, the most skilful, the most honorable of the daguerreotype professors do hail Mr. Hill's discovery with enthusiasm, and honor the discoverer. But, alas! it is also true that there are in the daguerreotype profession, some who are not only a disgrace to their profession, but to human nature itself. Some of these have been the most prominent in intruding on his privacy, in throwing before the public insulting inuendoes as well as positive falsehoods, harassing him with diabolical threats, &c. But I forbear at present. There is a chapter in the history of this discovery which, for the honor of humanity, I will hope may not be required to be given, but, if necessary, shall be given, for the purpose at least of showing the nature of the trials to which our American discoverer has been subjected. Mr. Hill has made a great discovery. It is not perfected. There is much yet to be done to make it perfect, but he is in advance of all others, and has within the year successfully overcome two of his difficulties. Both yellow and white were defective in quality and truth a year ago; both are now comparatively obtained. There are other colors which, in order to make them so true as to satisfy an artist's mind will require yet further experimenting. Is not this reason enough for not at present giving his process to the public? Who has a right to demand him to reveal it to the public now? Who, indeed, has a right to demand it at any time? I trust his life may be spared not only to perfect his process, but that he may reap some reward, both in honor and in profit, for his labors before death shall take him from us.

With respect, gentlemen, your most obedient servant,

SAM'L F. B. MORSE.

Poughkeepsie, New York, Oct. 4, 1852.

In addition to the foregoing, I have been favored with more than fifty similar statements from persons of the first standing in society. Of many of these I present abstracts. As their republication forms a part of the legitimate history of Heliochromy, I trust they will be read with interest.

The following extracts from a letter of P. C. White, Esq,, published in the *Cincinnati Daily Times*, of August 25, show the opinion of a portrait painter of high standing :—

You ask me why I do not return to Cincinnati. The time has not yet come. Suffice it to say for the present, that I have been out to see the Hillotype, or photograph in natural colors, discovered by L. L. Hill, and that until it comes out, I shall not feel disposed to leave New York. I have seen several pictures taken by the camera.

These pictures are enameled—cannot be rubbed out—can be seen from any point of view—as easily taken as daguerreotypes—not any more expensive—have most of the charms of natural color—will prove a great auxiliary to art—and are a contribution of wondrous beauty to the science of the age. The colors are a discovery—the process of taking them an invention, destined by the science of our time to advance and popularize æsthetic study beyond all former precedent.

This is an American contribution to science for the next World's Fair, to which European schools of art will be more indebted than they have been to Greece. Now, in this democracy of science—the true vicegerent of the Divine Master, infallible and superhuman—we have a reliable master, not of fabulous descent from Jupiter, but of demonstrable descent from the Father of Light, revealing and verifying the true, exposing the false, and suggesting that spiritual ideal that ravishes the true student of nature.

Nor are its utilitarian aspects to be overlooked; for Mr. Hill is a public benefactor, deserving riches and immortality. He has furnished to the widow and the fatherless, and those that have no help, a truly feminine and reliable profession; and to the traveller, the man of science, the botanist, florist, &c., a most valuable assistance.

WESTKILL, *Greene Co., N. Y., Dec.* 12, 1851.

I take great pleasure in stating that Mr. L. L. Hill has been well known in this community for many years; that for eight or nine years he served the church of which I am pastor, in the same sacred capacity—and that his character for moral honesty and integrity stands far above suspicion; so much so, that no one who is intimately acquainted with him would believe him capable of practising deception upon the public by professing to have made a great and important discovery which he did not know, beyond the possibility of "a delusion" or mistake, he could at the proper time prove, to the conviction of the most skeptical.

I know from personal inspection, that his avowed discovery is "an unmitigated" reality, having repeatedly examined many of his pictures heliotyped in natural colors, upon burnished silver plates, chemically coated; and which present, in a beautiful and brilliant form, the various shades and tints of red, blue, violet, green, yellow, orange, and all the colors of the spectrum.

The specimens which I have examined consist not only of copies of colored prints, but flowers, views, and likenesses of persons whom I know, taken from life, and surpassing, in a degree far beyond expression, the finest miniature paintings I have ever seen.

I have no personal interest to subserve in making this avowal, but do it from the purest motives, and with a sincere desire to aid in vindicating the character of Mr. Hill from the many invidious attacks made upon it, by persons who seem to be ignorant of his high moral worth, as well as of the reality and transcendent character of his discovery—assured, that, so soon as he is able to perfect the subordinate details to the satisfaction of his own mind, and so as to render his process simple and intelligible to the practitioners of the Daguerrean art, he will submit the brilliant results to the scrutinizing inspection of an intelligent public.

A. E. CLARK,
Pastor of the Baptist Church, Westkill.

From S. S. Harding, Esq., portrait painter, and brother of the celebrated artist Chester Harding, Boston. S. S. Harding is well known in many parts of the United States as a gentleman eminent in his profession.

ALBION, N. Y. *Nov.* 21, 1851.

REV. MR. HILL—DEAR SIR:—Your letter of the 17th has just this moment been received, and I hasten cheerfully to comply with your request. How any one could be malicious enough to say that such pictures as you were kind enough to show us were transferred, is past my comprehension; and base must be the man who could throw any obstacle in the way of your progress in this wonderful discovery.

S. S. HARDING.

I fully concur in the above.

S. M. HARVEY,
Daguerreotypist, Albion.

CATSKILL, *Greene Co., N. Y., Jan.* 27, 1851.

TO THE PUBLIC:—This certifies that I have been privileged to be a witness to the discovery of L. L. Hill, and I take great pleasure in stating, in the most positive terms, that having seen a large number of his specimens, they are better by far, than he has ever represented them, being far superior to the best Daguerreotypes or Paintings. His views possess a charm, which no pencil or brush can equal, and which nature alone can excel. His portraits from life, in natural colors, are perfectly exquisite. The tints of the various complexions are beautifully natural, soft, and harmonious; the rosy hues of the cheeks and lips, the color of the eyes, hair, and the various tints of red, blue, green, orange, violet, buff, &c., in the drapery, greatly surpass the utmost I have ever conceived from the published accounts. A chief beauty of these pictures is in the blue, green, fawn, and other colored grounds; these presenting a sort of mellow, illuminated appearance, which causes the portrait to set out with a surprising relief and life-like aspect. In a word, I cheerfully lend my name to the assertion that Mr. Hill's claim is true, to the fullest extent.

GEORGE W. HALCOTT,
Sheriff of Greene Co., N. Y.

ROCHESTER, *Monroe Co., May* 14, 1852.

This certifies that I have seen great numbers of the results of L. L. Hill's process for photographing in natural colors, and I take great pleasure in affirming most positively that they are all, and more than he ever represented them. They are natural colors in every possible variety, including red, blue, yellow, orange, buff, fawn, brown, green, &c., embracing the minutest middle tints of every hue. The portraits from life are marvellous productions, and no man of taste can see them without feeling that a great light has arisen in the mountain wilds of Westkill. Mr. Hill has made a wonderful discovery, one that will supersede every other form of coloration. The beautiful lights and shades of Daguerreotypes will now give way to these more beautiful blendings of the prismatic rays. I cannot speak too highly of the portraits from life, which Mr. Hill was kind enough to show me. One, of a person with whose features I am well acquainted, I must say, baffles description. It exhibits the fresh tints, the color of the cheeks, lips, hair, and drapery, with a softness and glossy brilliancy beyond conception, and yet this transcript of life itself, standing out on a soft, colored ground, is most remarkable for its perfect resemblance to life. May God speed the pleasing wonder!

JAMES HEATH, *Daguerreotypist,*
55 Emporium Block, Main street, Rochester.

NEW YORK, *Dec.* 20, 1851.

This certifies that Mr. Hill has kindly shown me several specimens of his pictures in natural colors. In justice to him I take great pleasure in expressing my admiration of these wonderful works of light, and in stating that they afford the most pleasing and conclusive evidence that Mr. Hill's claim to his magnificent discovery is a just one. He showed to me, among other specimens, copies of paintings, smaller than the originals, which I saw, proving them to have been taken in a Camera; also, a rose bush, a wreath of roses, and various other specimens of this truly surprising discovery, in all of which the colors were well defined and properly located. I also saw a portrait from life, on a half size plate, which was strikingly beautiful. As one whose whole soul is in the photographic art, I feel a just pride in stating that the above picture is all sufficient and glorious proof of the great importance of Mr. Hill's discovery, and a complete vindication of the truth of his pretensions from the first.

Mr. Hill has confidentially explained to me, as an operator, some of his reasons for not publicly exhibiting his pictures. These reasons are perfectly satisfactory, and lead him to act as any man would who regarded the safety of his discovery.

SAMUEL ROOT, *Daguerrean Artist*,
363 Broadway, New York.

PHILADELPHIA, *Jan.* 6, 1852.

I have seen Mr. L. L. Hill's finished pictures, portraits from life, taken with the Camera, upon silver surfaces, or usual Daguerreotype plates, and must say, in reference to their perfect exactness of transcription from their originals, and their exquisite, their transcendent beauty, as works of art, I can not only endorse all he has said of them, but would speak even more strongly, if stronger language could be found.

I have also seen numerous specimens of Mr. Hill's "experiments," produced by the action of light, such as copies of prints, flowers, &c., with a view of developing the various shades, or tints of colors, many of which were truly beautiful and interesting.

His portraits from life, I am happy to say, are all that the most enthusiastic Daguerrean Artist can desire, and much more beautiful than our scientific men and the public have been led to suppose. The time will come when all generous minds will award to Mr. Hill due credit for having guarded so faithfully, thus far, the wonderful discovery which it has been his good fortune to bring before the world.

M. A. ROOT, *Daguerreotypist*,
140 Chestnut street, Philadelphia.

NEW YORK, June 12, 1852.

This is to certify that I have just visited Mr. L. L. Hill, at his residence, and that he gratified me with a sight of his pictures in natural colors. I say most cheerfully, and as an act of justice to Mr. Hill, that I am perfectly satisfied of the truth of his claim in the broadest and fullest sense. These pictures are really exquisite and beautiful, differing essentially from any other style of picture. They present every possible variety of color and tint, in a most brilliant form—the whites are peculiarly bright and glossy—and the aspect of the pictures is one of astonishing boldness and relief. The flesh tints of the pictures from life, the color of the hair, drapery, background, &c., are fine beyond description; and I unhesitatingly pronounce the invention a wonderful one, and shall hail with joy the day when I shall be allowed to work it.

J. GURNEY,
189 Broadway, N. Y.

NEW YORK, July 5, 1852.

I cheerfully concur in the foregoing, and would add stronger language, if stronger could be found, in support of the entire, and most gratifying truth of Mr. Hill's discovery. From actual inspection of his results—among them portraits from life—I am amazed and delighted beyond my power to express.

C. C. HARRISON, *Camera Manufacturer*,
85 Duane street, N. Y.

Mr. Harrison is one of the oldest and best Daguerreotypists in the country; and as a practical optician, has gained a world-wide fame in the manufacture of Cameras.

BOSTON, August 30, 1252.

This is to certify that I have examined with astonishment, several Daguerreotypes, in which were faithfully copied all the colors of nature, by L. L. Hill, among them a portrait from life, and upwards of thirty different copies of colored engravings; and I am fully convinced that he has discovered a chemical process by which he can take Daguerreotypes with all the natural colors. Many of those shown me were copies of birds of paradise; the subjects being a capital test for his newly discovered art; in the copies is represented upon the silver plates, every shade and tint of color imaginable; the impression is more readily seen than in the common Daguerreotype, and appears imbedded *in* the silver, instead of being upon the surface; and the higher the plate is polished, after the impression is taken, the more brilliant are the colors thrown out.

JOHN A. WHIPPLE, *Daguerreotypist*,
96 Washington street, Boston.

ST. LOUIS, MO., Sept. 15, 1852.

Friend Whipple, in the above, has told the truth; for I have seen the same.

E. LONG,
S. E. corner 4th and Market street.

OTSEGO, N. Y., March 10, 1852.

Having examined a number of Mr. Hill's specimens, I hereby certify, that his daily experiments show rapid and marked advancement in the art, which betoken a speedy consummation. Having also examined some of his portraits, from life, in natural colors, I certify that my best anticipations were more than realized. According to my judgment, they far surpass in beauty, truthfulness, and finish, any engraving or painting ever examined by me, leaving nothing more to be desired in the way of portrait taking.

ERASTUS WESTCOTT,
Pastor Baptist Church.

PRATTSVILLE, N. Y., Aug. 19, 1852.

This certifies that I have seen L. L. Hill's portraits from life, and other specimens in natural colors, and they are beautiful beyond the power of language to describe. They afford the most positive proof of the truth of his assertions respecting the greatness and utility of his discovery. I also certify, to the country and the world at large, that I have known Mr. Hill many years, and his integrity is as natural and real as the glowing colors on his plates.

JOHN LARAWAY,
Former Sheriff of Greene Co.

LEXINGTON, May 25, 1852.

This certifies that I have seen numerous specimens of the results of Mr. L. L. Hill's process of photographing in colors. Incredible as it may seem, it is strictly true that these pictures, and especially the portraits of living persons, are all, and more than language has ever described them. His process gives not only every color, but the minutest tint of every color, and that with a brilliant, enameled appearance, truly charming and exquisitely soft and beautiful. I could not speak too strongly of these wonderful pictures, and especially would my words be inadequate to describe the charm of the flesh color and carnation tint of the portraits from life.

D. LYMAN,
Minister of the Gospel, Methodist Ep. Church.

LEXINGTON, N. Y., Jan. 2, 1851.

In the portraits and views there is all that Mr. Hill has represented to the public; and I may add, a truthfulness to the colors of the complexion, hair, eyes, drapery, back-ground, &c., and a certain peculiar appearance, as of life itself, which no man's language can adequately represent.

HEZEKIAH PETTIT,
Pastor of the Baptist Church in Lexington for fifty years past.

NEW YORK, Gurney's Gallery, 189 Broadway, May 24, 1852.

I have seen Mr. L. L. Hill's pictures in natural colors, and examined them with the closest scrutiny in broad daylight; and I unhesitatingly certify to the existence of the discovery in a most desirable shape. I can conceive of nothing more perfect than these pictures, and the process will most certainly supersede all others the instant it is introduced. I have the honor of being the first person that visited Mr. Hill in reference to his discovery—have frequently visited Westkill, and must say, that though I do not know anything of a perfect man, I never knew a man who enjoyed the love and confidence of his neighbors more than the slandered L. L. Hill.

CALEB HUNT, *Daguerreotypist.*

GRANVILLE, O., Sept. 1, 1852.

I hereby certify that I have seen and carefully examined Mr. L. L. Hill's pictures taken in natural colors, and that they far exceed in richness, depth, boldness, relief, and mellowness of tone, the finest daguerreotype or oil painting, and at the same time display all the tints of every variety of color. If the fraternity do not trouble him too much with visits and propositions, he will soon introduce the process in a very desirable and practical shape.

Yours truly, W. H. WEEKS, *Daguerreotypist.*

For three years with M. A. Root, Philadelphia.

ASHLAND, N. Y., Nov. 12, 1851.

Some months since I saw several specimens of L. L. Hill's photography in natural colors, and would say, with pleasure, that they bear no marks of being transfers, but are the true colors of the objects from which they were taken by the action of light, through the medium of the Camera Obscura.

MORRIS BAILEY, *Daguerreotypist.*

Now of 88 Merrimac street, Lowell, Mass.

CATSKILL, Dec. 2, 1851.

We, the undersigned, being well acquainted with Mr. Morris Bailey, would say that we believe him to be a man of strict honor and integrity, and that any statement that he has made, or shall make, may be relied upon by the public.

GEORGE W. HALCOTT,

Sheriff of Greene County, N. Y.

J. VAN ORDEN, *Clerk of Do.*

NEWBURG, N. Y., Nov. 27, 1851.

I certify that I have seen many of L. L. Hill's pictures in natural colors. I have spent much time at his house, and repeatedly seen him produce, by means of the Camera, copies of colored prints and paintings which were exceedingly accurate representations of the originals. I have also seen his portraits from life, which are exceedingly beautiful; and in two instances I saw him take portraits of living persons, with very short sittings (only a few seconds), in which all the colors of the complexion and dress were beautifully rendered.

WM. SCHERMERHORN, *Daguerreotypist.*

From the Newburgh Gazette, Oct. 20, 1852.

THE WONDERS OF THE HILLOTYPE.

We have been shown by Mr. Hill, the inventor of the "Hillotype," a variety of the beautiful creations of his genius. He has really invented a process of transferring to his plates all the natural colors. The freshness of life is imparted to his pictures, which are not excelled in their resemblance of nature, even by the gorgeous tints of the rainbow. Red, and Blue, and Yellow, the principal primary colors, are copied with wonderful facility by his truly marvellous invention, and with them are mingled, with perfect exactness, all the various hues and tints, and combinations of colors of the solar spectrum. We could scarcely believe that a "consummation so devoutly to be wished," had been reached, until we beheld it, as we have had the happiness of doing, with our own eyes. Now that we have seen it, like "unbelieving Thomas," we are entirely satisfied of its actuality.

But we have not the space at present to particularize the merits of this invention. Mr. Hill is about making arrangements to perfect his discovery, and give the world the benefit of its extraordinary capabilities. The public, we are sure, will hail the day, which is fast approaching, when their curiosity, equally with their wants, can be gratified with the inspection as well as the possession of his exact and beautiful imitations of the prismatic colors.

KINGSTON, N. Y., Dec. 27, 1851.

This certifies, that some months ago, I was kindly favored by my old and well-tried friend, Mr. L. L. Hill, with a sight of several specimens of his pictures in natural colors. Those I saw were evidently a great improvement in the art—exhibiting as they did, in a clear, distinct, and brilliant manner, the several colors and tints of the solar spectrum. Of the copies of colored prints I saw, I examined the originals, and found them much larger than the copies, settling the matter conclusively that these specimens of Mr. Hill's matchless discovery were produced in the Camera.

Mr. Hill has also shown me some pictures from life, in which the colors are rendered with a truthfulness truly surprising.

DANIEL BRADBURY,
Formerly Publisher of the Rondout Freeman.

KINGSTON, N. Y., *Dec.* 27, 1851.

This certifies that we are well acquainted with Mr. Daniel Bradbury, and that his character for moral worth, truth, and integrity, is fully established in our minds, and in this community.

WM. H. ROMEYN, *P. M.*
J. D. L. MONTAYNE, *Clerk of Ulster Co.*
WILLIAM MASTEN, *Surrogate.*
THOS. CLARK, *County Treasurer.*

KINGSTON, N. Y. Nov. 24, 1851.

This certifies that I have witnessed several of Mr. L. L. Hill's experiments in natural colors. I saw him produce, photogenically, beautiful copies of colored objects, by an exposure of three or four seconds to diffuse light. I saw the originals, and state positively, that they were copied true to the tints of color, including various shades of green, red, blue, orange, and yellow. Having through this medium my imagination fired in relation to the beauty of his chief productions, I must say that it was totally submerged in the reality that was exhibited to my view in the portraits from life.

JOSEPH W. KERR.

In the truth and integrity of Joseph W. Kerr, we have full confidence.

C. S. CLAY, *Druggist.*
JAS. S. SMITH, *Pres. Kingston Bank.*
M. SCHOONMAKER, *Att'y at Law.*
R. N. BALDWIN, *Merchant.*

The subjoined article, from the *Rondout Examiner*, written by the talented editor of that paper, Robert Gosman, Esq., I give entire, for the reason that Mr. Gosman has said for me what I could not so well express myself.

From the Rondout Examiner of June 3, 1852.

THE HILLOTYPE—ITS DISCOVERY, PROGRESS, AND POSITION.

Some eighteen months ago the world was pleasantly surprised by the announcement that the Rev. L. L. Hill, of Westkill, Greene County, New York, had mastered a secret which had baffled all inquisitive science up to that time, viz. the art of "Daguerreotyping in colors." It was stated in a communication by Mr. Hill to a journal specially devoted to Daguerrean art, that the only material obstacle to full success seemed to be in the inability to reproduce the yellow tints of the original. Of course so near an approach to complete discovery, which hundreds in this country and Europe had been seeking without achieving anything, made quite a sensation.

It is proper to say here that the "Hillotype" was the name given to the production of Mr. Hill's process, by a journal devoted to Daguerrean information. And it is but justice to say, too, that Mr. Hill's discovery was not a stumble upon an unsought art, but that he had been earnestly engaged some two years in pursuit of the secret, which burst upon him when he least looked for the revelation.

Mr. Hill, on the announcement as above, was an object of general attention, and especially so to the Daguerreotypists generally. His secluded abode was overrun by visitors, and he was as suddenly overwhelmed by letters. There were some visitors and inquirers who had a rational curiosity to satisfy, but the major part were persons exercising the Daguerrean art mechanically, and anxious to gain the process for the pecuniary gains which certainly would follow its first exercise. The consequence was, that Mr. Hill was almost deprived of the time to pursue his labors for the completion of his art, and annoyed beyond endurance by some of his sordid and prying visitors, who stood upon no considerations of delicacy in pursuing their purpose. There were those, it is true, among visitors and correspondents, who were of a different mould, and who showed their sympathy by proffers of aid in any desired shape. But Mr. Hill had a very natural and honorable desire to complete his discovery alone, and hence he was compelled to decline many kind offices of this class, though sensible of their worth.

His position at this time (one year ago) was peculiar. He labored alone. His means of support, as well as the funds for his large outlay for materials, were derived from the sale of a treatise on the Daguerrean art, forming a manual for the operator, added to something derived from the tuition of pupils. This was certainly not the most agreeable situation for an enthusiastic pursuit, but Mr. Hill was satisfied. He pursued his studies with intensity, scarcely allowing himself time for sleep. He was compelled to fix stringent rules as to visitants, and warned by some very flagrant inquisitions, he was also forced to deny ordinary visitants a sight of his results.

At this time (the summer of 1851), Mr. Hill was sanguine of the completion of his discovery in a few weeks. Obstacles, however, prevented this, but his progress was such as to give him strong hope from day to day of final success. In November, 1851, Westkill was invaded by a self-styled Convention from a "State Daguerrean Association," whose proceedings may, possibly, be the subject of another notice. It is enough now to say, that the conduct of the master-spirit of the three inquisitors was such that Mr. Hill declined showing them his plates, or giving them that satisfaction which was demanded as a right. This "Committee" published a report in a New York paper, signed by five names, though but three persons were at Mr. Hill's residence. The gist of the report was, that Mr. Hill had not only deluded others, but himself, and that the whole history of his alleged discovery, "has been an unmitigated delusion." The "Committee," however, very contradictorily charged Mr. Hill with making a profit of his alleged pretense—a charge which, it is plain, would rather militate against the after admission of his "delusion." They averred in fact, that from the sale of his books and tuition of pupils attracted by the fame of his discovery, he "realized a handsome income," and that this was the real object of Mr. Hill's announcement.

This report—characterless, and bearing on its face the most sordid and narrow motives—did injure Mr. Hill materially. Where he was personally known it could do him no harm. But the first announcement of his discovery had injured the Daguerrean business sensibly, and operators eagerly seized and circulated a denial which might avail their interests. The result was, Mr. Hill's treatise was no longer a source of revenue to him, and he was compelled, in self-vindication, to dismiss his pupils. But the worst effect was the sore blow given to a sensitive, nervous man, not very well hardened at best by contact with this bustling world, and unstrung by intense solitary labor and seclusion. Conscious of his rectitude of purpose, and the validity of his discovery, he was hurt by imputations of this sordid cast. He did, however, sustained by personal friends knowing his integrity, and by artists able to certify to the truth of his productions, interpose a defence against this assault. But the mischief had been done in begetting a skepticism which those interested in it knew how to turn to account. And though among those who came to the rescue he might include Professor Morse, and other adepts in sciences, and of the most unquestioned integrity, yet the world looked on with indifference for the time, whilst Mr. Hill pursued his solitary struggles towards success.

During the whole of the pendency of Mr. Hill's discovery, the writer of this article has had the firmest faith in its actuality, based on a knowledge of Mr. Hill's science years ago, and the reports of reliable witnesses who had verified his pretences by sight.

The "Committee report" was too transparent and common a newspaper "speculation" to impose upon any one experienced in the doublings of journalism, and it would have been a weak part indeed to have been imposed upon by such a mass of discrepancies.

Having a natural curiosity to see a "Hillotype," the writer would probably have visited Westkill a year ago, but for the impression that it would only retard Mr. Hill's progress, and infringe upon a time already too much trespassed upon by the curious. But circumstances allowing a visit, divested of its intrusive character, the writer a few days ago had the privilege of visiting Mr. Hill's studio, and will state what he saw there.

A VISIT TO WESTKILL—MR. HILL AND HIS HILLOTYPES.

On the morning of the 24th of May, the writer with a friend, visited Mr. Hill's studio at Westkill. After some conversation Mr. Hill exhibited some dozen or more "Hillotypes" on large sized plates. They were the copies of elaborately colored French engravings. In these, the most diversified and delicate hues and tints were rendered with the most beautiful distinctness. It was especially noted by the writer that all shades of yellow (Mr. Hill had been puzzled by this color at his outset) running through all gradations from the richest aureole to the faintest tint in a complexion, were freely and transparently rendered. These specimens (indiscriminately taken from Mr. Hill's more recent experiments) showed every conceivable combination of the original colors, many of the prints being colored solely with reference to the exhibitions of contrasts, combinations, and shades.

Besides these, the writer saw four Hillotypes from life, preserving all the colors of nature. One of the cameo size was a fine female head, with the hair in Jenny Lind style, and the other, the same head in a green silk bonnet, the most minute colors in the dress being given to the life. These two portraitures were exquisitely natural in color, and the subject was a fine looking specimen of the mountain girl, in all the bloom of vigorous youth. But the lack of knowledge of the original which to these was a drawback to a full appreciation, as well as that of a fine portrait of an elderly woman, could not be pleaded as to the fourth, which was a Hillotype, on a larger plate, of the artist's daughter, a child of some two years old.

This latter, the writer regarded as an ample vindication of Mr. Hill's claims in their widest sense. In want of a subject one morning, Mr. H. requested the mother to bring in the child. A variegated table-cover was hastily thrown over a trunk, and the child, taking an easy recumbent position, in a few seconds was depicted upon the plate with all the force of nature. By fortunate accident all the more vivid tints of red, green, and blue, were included in the dress and accessories, and scanning the portrait beside the child, left the writer no ground for skepticism as to the consummation of the discovery. The complexion, the very peculiar tint of the hair, the color of the eyes, nay, the faint pink of the finger tips, were all there, mirrored in all the freshness of breathing life.

The writer will add, that the uncovered plates were put in his hands for the most rigid examination, by the full light of an unclouded summer day. And one which had not been burnished, was put to that process in his presence, when it took, in an instant, the rich enamel-like surface, which distinctly marks the Hillotype from the Daguerreotype. The fact is (as we saw from experiment), the Hillotype is very difficult to remove from the plate as compared with the Daguerreotype, nor is it sensitive to the effect of atmosphere like the latter.

This statement is sufficient, we presume, so far as the evidence of a witness can establish a fact of this kind. Other corroborative and explanatory statements might be made, but the writer has no idea of imperilling Mr. Hill's secret in the most remote degree, by stating anything beyond the line of effects to which he could testify without hesitation on any score.

The writer closes this statement with the hope that Mr. Hill will be one of the exceptions to the rule, that inventors do not reap the reward of their genius. He has met the most discouraging obstacles in his labors, and has overcome them with heroism. That he can pronounce his work well nigh accomplished, and that it will soon be given to the world, the writer believes. And it ought to be remembered, to the praise of the inventor too, that he has carried on all his operations alone; every process down to the merest mechanical operations, having been accomplished single-handed.

I append the following, because it will show the opinion of my neighbors.

From the Prattsville Advocate, Jan. 17, 1852.

THE HILLOTYPE.

On Tuesday last, we, in company with a friend, availed ourselves of the pleasure of visiting the Rev. Mr. Hill, at his residence in Westkill, in this county, for the double purpose of seeing his specimens, and satisfying ourselves whether his discovery was in truth such as would stand the scrutinizing test of time, or whether it was emphatically a humbug—and, reader, here permit us to say, that we acknowledge that we had been assured by good authority, that in truth his discovery was all that he claimed it to be—but these statements fell far short of the reality. If we ever had any misgivings on the subject, they have for ever passed from our mind; for what we saw with our own eyes, we must believe. Of Mr. Hill, all who have the pleasure of an acquaintance with him, will agree with us in saying, that humbuggery forms no part of his character—that on his countenance are plainly seen the marks of ingenuousness—that he is far above playing the contemptible game of catchpenny. He has a mass of evidence in his possession which will soon be given to the world, from eminent Daguerreian artists and scientific men, establishing his right to the discovery—and from men who have spent years and years in attempting to find out the grand secret whereby he can, in a life-like manner, present to the eye of the astonished beholder, colors true to nature; for instance, a blackberry bush, with every leaf fresh, as if now grown in its native soil, the stalk, the blossom, the green and ripe fruit, all perfect in color—all blended as harmoniously as the peerless art of Nature itself reveals them to our eye. We hazard nothing in saying that his discovery will be the crowning effort of the Daguerrean Art, and his fame is destined to outlive the noisy swarm of "little fry," who now pour out their anathemas upon him for accomplishing that which their genius can never attain, much less excel. While their names and acts shall be sunk in the muddy pool of oblivion, his will be classed with that of Franklin, Fulton, and other benefactors of mankind.

His natural pictures, or rather his copies from nature, bear a more perfect resemblance to the original, than anything ever yet emanating from the pencil of the most accomplished artist. This is also emphatically true of the portraits of living persons taken by Mr. Hill, many of which we recognised. Every lineament of the face was clearly defined; there was a truthfulness and beauty in them which the most world-renowned artist has never as yet been able to produce. No sane person will attempt to controvert the position that daguerreotypes are (or have been) the most perfect likenesses it is possible to obtain of the "human face divine," the process by which they are obtained admitting of not the slightest variation, but the crowning glory of the Hillotype consists in the truthfulness of feature and expression, a softness, a brilliancy of tone, and nicety of shading hitherto unparalleled. These portraits are not easily defaced; and our attempt to mar their beauty only served to brighten them, and to more clearly portray their matchless elegance.

We are not surprised that there are skeptics in regard to this matter—it is matter of wonder that there are not more—but we are none of them. Our eyes have seen, and we cannot do otherwise than believe. May a kind Providence grant him health and strength to complete (to his entire satisfaction, not ours, for we confess we thought them perfect) his glorious art.

In addition to the foregoing, I could present at least five hundred similar statements. I have shown my results to more than one thousand persons, never to my knowledge without exciting admiration. For years my house has been almost literally overrun with visitors from various parts of the world; and although I have been thereby greatly hindered, their words of cheer as they gazed upon my pictures, have been no slight incentive to perseverance. Among the vast number who have inspected my results, I have never known one case of dissatisfaction. Those who have spent much time in my house, and have seen for themselves the working of the process, have continued to this day my warmest friends.

It would be exceedingly gratifying to my own feelings to enter more largely into this subject; but I must not forget that I am writing a "Treatise on Heliochromy," and that I am to "stick to my text." It shall be my aim throughout this work to justify the title I have given it. A proper understanding of the subject, as well as justice to myself, seemed to require the above rather lengthy argument in support of my claim. For the present I will dismiss M. Niepce de St. Victor, promising to give a full and fair exposition of his process in a future chapter.

CHAPTER V.

Various Processes—Sir John Herschel's Anthotype—Robert Hunt's Processes—Ferrocyanide paper—Bi.-Chromate of Potash—Hydriodated Paper—Copying a green Leaf—M. Edmund Becquerel's process—M. Niepce de Saint Victor's process—These processes fully and fairly detailed.

I.—SIR JOHN HERSCHEL'S ANTHOTYPE.

The interesting facts brought out by this great man's experiments demand a further investigation. A very few words, however, will give an idea of his processes. He operated on the colored juices of flowers and grapes. The Corchorus Japonica, the Ten Week Stocks, Papaver Orientale, Viola Odorata, Red Poppy, and Senecio Splendens, were the principal flowers he employed. "Such parts of these flowers as possessed a uniform tint, were crushed to a pulp in a marble mortar, either alone, or with addition of alcohol, and the juice expressed by squeezing the pulp in a clean linen or cotton cloth. It was then spread on paper and gently dried. Under a superimposed engraving these papers were exposed to the light, for a period ranging from half an hour to one month." There is a difficulty in respect to the alcohol, since, in many cases, if it is not employed the color of the juice is irrecoverably destroyed, and the employment of it retards the action of the light. The alcohol effects a temporary destruction of the color, in many cases, but the color re-appears on drying the paper.

The above brief account of Herschel's method of operating will enable any ingenious person to pursue this line of research. But, although Sir John did obtain some tintings of color in the use of these vegetable juices, I have described other methods of using them which give far better results.

II.—SIR ROBERT HUNT'S PROCESSES.

PROCESS No. 1. Wash highly glazed paper with a solution of nitrate of silver of the strength of one drachm of the salt to one oz. water. Dry quickly, and repeat the wash. Dry as before, and place the paper for a minute in a solution of iodide of potash—1 drachm to 3 oz. water. Wash gently with water. To sensitize, wash the paper with a solution of ferrocyanate of potash—1 drachm to 3 oz. water. Expose wet.

On such paper Mr. Hunt obtained, once, a tolerably good colored image of the solar spectrum.

PROCESS No. 2. A tolerably strong solution of bi-chromate of potash is the first wash for the paper. Dry and wash with a very weak solution of nitrate of silver. Exposed under colored glasses for two days, it became tinted a blue, a green, and a red.

PROCESS No. 3. Soak the paper a few minutes in a muriated wash—say common salt (muriate of soda) and dry. Wash this with a solution of nitrate of silver—say 60 grains to 1 oz. water, and instantly expose to sunshine, until it darkens as much as it will. Repeat the wash, and expose to the sun until it comes to a fine chocolate brown. A hydriodate of potash, soda, ammonia, manganese, or baryta—say 30 grains to 1 oz. water—is now washed over the darkened paper. The paper is to be used wet. With colored fluids superimposed Mr. Hunt obtained the complementary colors of violet, blue, green, yellow, and red.

PROCESS No. 4. Place a green leaf on a polished Daguerreotype plate, and hold it down by a piece of glass. Pour upon it, so that the plate may be covered, a solution of the hydriodate of potash, containing a little free iodine: then expose the whole to sunshine. In about half an hour a copy is obtained. This results from the action of the yellow rays producing their complementary color—green; which is evident from the solution being yellow, and not, therefore, permitting the passage of the green rays.

III.—M. EDMUND BECQUEREL'S PROCESS.

Terminate the copper pole of a Daniels battery with a plate of platina. To the terminating wire of the zinc pole attach a plate of silver, or daguerreotype plate, and immerse both in a jar of muriatic acid, diluted one half with water. When the plate arrives at a violet color, the second time rinse with water and dry. This process gives by a very prolonged exposure some colors, but fails to produce more than one or two at once, and these not brilliant, Besides, they fade even in diffuse light.

IV.—M. NIEPCE DE SAINT VICTOR'S PROCESS.

I give this process entire, for several reasons, the most important of which is that my reader may compare it with my diary, given in a subsequent chapter, in which it will be seen that long before M. Niepce's discovery, I used the chlorides, and obtained colors, but gave up the process as impracticable and insufficient; and yet, that these very experiments led on to the discovery of many other processes, and to the process upon which I finally settled, and which I announced to the world.

The memoir of M. Niepce, before the French Academy, is entitled, "The relation existing between the colors of certain colored flames, with the Heliographic images colored by light."

When a plate of silver is plunged into a solution of sulphate of copper and chloride of sodium at the same time that it is rendered *electro-positive* by means of the voltaic battery, the chloride formed becomes susceptible of coloration, when, having been withdrawn from the bath, it receives the influence of light. This was the discovery of Becquerel. M. Niepce had been led to think that a relation existed between the color communicated by a body to a flame, and the color developed upon a plate of silver, which should have been chloridated with the body which colors this flame. The bath in which the plate of silver was plunged, was formed of water saturated with chlorine, to which was added a chloride possessing the property of coloring flame.

It is well known that strontia gives a purple color to flames in general, and to that of alcohol in particular. If we prepare a plate of silver and pass it into water saturated with chlorine, to which is added some chloride of strontia, and when thus prepared we place it upon a colored design, of red and other colors, and then expose it to the sunshine, after six or seven minutes we shall perceive that the colors of the image are reproduced upon the plate, but the reds much more decidedly than the others. When we would produce successfully the other rays of the solar spectrum, we operate in the same manner we have indicated for the red ray, employing for the orange the chloride of calcium, or that of uranium for the yellow, or hypochlorite of soda, or the chloride of sodium and potassium. If we plunge a plate of silver in the chlorine liquid, or if we expose the plate to the vapor, we obtain all the colors by the light, but the yellow only with any degree of veracity. Very fine yellows have been obtained with a bath composed of water slightly acidulated with hydrochloric acid with a salt of copper. The green rays are obtained with boracic acid, or the chloride of nickel; also with all the salts of copper. The blue rays are obtained with the double chloride of copper and ammonia. Indigo rays are obtained with the same. The violet rays are obtained with the chloride of strontia and the sulphate of copper.

All the substances which give colored flames, give also colored images by the light. If we take any of the substances which do not give color to the flame, we do not obtain colored images by the light; we produce upon the plate a negative image, composed merely of black and white, as in the ordinary photographs. Those substances which give white flames, as the chlorides of antimony, lead, and zinc, yield no color by luminous action. All the colors of the picture have been produced by preparing a bath composed of the deuto-chloride of copper; this salt thrown into burning alcohol produces a variegated flame, according to the intensity of the fire; and it is nearly the same with all the salts of copper mixed with chlorine. If we put a salt of copper in chlorine liquid, we obtain a very sensitive surface by a single immersion; but the result of this mixture is seldom good. I prefer taking the deuto-chloride of copper, to which I add three or four pounds of water: this bath gives good results. A mixture of equal parts of chloride of copper and chloride of iron, with three or four parts of water, is, however, the best. The chloride of iron has, like that of copper, the property of being impressed on the plate of silver, and of producing many colors; but they are infinitely more feeble, and the yellow always predominates; this agrees with the yellow color produced in flame by chloride of iron. If we form a bath composed of all the substances which separately give a dominant color, we obtain very lively colors; but the great difficulty is the mixing in proper proportions, for it happens, nearly always, that some colors are found excluded by others. By care, however, we ought to arrive at the reproduction of all the colors. There exist many difficulties, more indeed than in any of the ordinary processes of photography. We cannot always depend upon obtaining the same results with the same materials, owing principally to the difficulty of preserving the solution at a uniform strength. Liquid chlorine is necessary; the application of dry chlorine will not produce the same result. The action of heat upon these prepared plates is, in some respects, analogous to the effects of light. By warming a plate over a spirit-lamp, we produce successively the following tints: brown red, a cerise red, scarlet, and red having a whitish tint. Numerous experiments have been made by M. Niepce to produce the colors upon the salts of silver and copper spread on paper, but hitherto without success; a metallic plate of silver—the plated copper answers—must be employed. Iodine and bromine, and their salts, have been tried, but they will not produce a surface capable of developing colors. Chlorine, in the state of chlorates or chlorides, is the only substance which possesses the property of being colored by light, when chemically combined with metallic silver.

"The plate being very highly polished, which is best effected by Tripoli powder and ammonia, is connected with the battery, and then plunged into the bath, and kept there for some minutes; it is then taken from the bath, washed in a large quantity of water, and dried over a spirit-lamp. The surface thus produced is a dull neutral tint, often almost black, and, upon exposing it to the light, the colors are produced by removing the blackness; the surface is, in fact, *eaten out in colors.* The sensibility of the plate appears to be increased by the action of heat, and when brought by the spirit-lamp to the cerise red color, it is in its most sensitive state. At present, however, the plate cannot be rendered very sensitive, two or three hours being required to produce a decided effect in the camera-obscura. It is, however, already found that the fluoride of sodium will very much accelerate the operation.

"The fixation of the colored image is, however, still a point of considerable difficulty, and, although a certain degree of permanence has been recovered, the colors fade out by exposure, and eventually pass away. A kind of lacquer appears to have been applied to the plates we have seen, and ordinary diffused light does not seem to produce much change upon them."—*London Athenæum.*

Thus I have given all the processes of which we have any published account; and I have done it the more cheerfully, because it places my discovery in its true light, and because a treatise like this would be incomplete without it. The reader may judge how far M. Niepce is entitled to credit for originality. After all the fuss that has been made about his great discovery,

I, for one, can see but one original idea in it, namely, the imaginary relation between the action of the colored rays and the colors of certain flames. The idea itself of chloridizing a silver plate he borrowed from Becquerel. He owns this in his "Memoir." What then has he originated? Here is the indisputable answer :—he has originated the use of various chlorides, for doing what Becquerel did with a few chlorides. I defy any man of sense to make any more than this out of his famous "Memoir." Yet this document has been paraded before the public in the natural colors which usually embellish envy and spite, with a view to depreciate an American invention. This has been done by men who became my enemies because I would not become their bosom friend, and let them have a bite at the "loaves and fishes." I could easily show up this account in items ; but it would be too personal a thing for a work like this ; and, what is more, the persons or creatures who have instigated and kept alive the flame of opposition against me, are not worthy of so much notice, and I prefer to leave them to sink into that "obscurity" they have wished for me.

CHAPTER VI.

CHEMISTRY OF HELIOCHROMY.

NATURAL COLORIFIC AGENTS.—*Esculent Vegetables.*—Carrots—Beets—Onions—Radishes—Squash—Pumpkin—Watermelon—Tomatoes—Lettuce—Cabbage—Red Peppers—Asparagus—Rhubarb—Sage. *Fruits.*—Peach—Cherry—Apple—Strawberry—Blackberry—Raspberry—Sumac Bobs—Currants—Grapes—Bittersweet—Sunflower Seeds—Pokeberries—Elderberries—Whortleberries—Squawberries. *Flowers*—Red Rose—Peony—Poppy—Dahlia—Marigold—Violet—Tiger Lily—Tulips—Peach Blows—Sky Rocket—Lilac—Dandelions—Daisies—St. John's Wort. *Grasses and Leaves.*—Red-top Clover—Ribbon Grass—Leaves of Willow—Sugar Maple—Peach—Butternut.

ARTIFICIAL COLORIFIC AGENTS.—*The Metals.*—Gold—Silver—Copper—Platina—Iron—Zinc—Lead—Antimony—Arsenic—Osmium—Iridium—Cobalt—Selenium—Mercury—Tin—Bismuth—Nickel—Potassium—Sodium—Aluminum—Their Alloys. *The Salts of Metals.*—Nitrate, Chloride, Bromide, Iodide, Fluoride, Ammoniuret, Fulminate, Citrate, Silvate, Cyanide, Hyposulphite, Phosphate, Carbonate, Borate, Chromate, and Alumina of Silver—Chlorides of Gold, Copper, Zinc, Lead, Iridium, Cobalt, &c.—Iodide and Bromide of Gold, Silver, Lead, &c.

THE ACIDS.—Nitric, Sulphuric, Sulphurous, Hydrochloric, Hydrofluoric, Citric, Iodic, Bromic, Tartaric, Uric, Gallic, Pyro-Gallic, Nitrous, Acetic, &c.

THE ALKALIES.—Soda, Baryta, Lime, and Strontia, and their combinations.

THE GASES AND VAPORS.—Chlorine, Hydrogen, Selenium, Phosphorous Vapor, Phosphuretted Hydrogen, Oxygen, Oxyde, Nitrous Oxyde, Hyponitric Acid Vapor.

IN this chapter I shall treat, first, of Natural Colorific Agents; viz., Esculent Vegetables, Fruits, Flowers, Leaves and Grasses.

It is an interesting fact, that many of the esculent vegetables are rich in heliochromic properties. The juices of many of them applied to paper, give, on exposure to light, some very curious results. Most of them contain coloring principles, which are acted upon in a powerful and singular manner by the solar spectrum. It is sufficient, in most cases, to press out the juice of the more colored parts, as the skin of the radish, the pulp of the tomato and watermelon, &c. If the liquid is to be preserved a length of time, it should be mixed with a little alcohol, and to every four ounces of the same you may add one drop of creosote. This will effectually preserve the liquid, and not injure, but rather exalt its heliochromic properties, by quickening the action of light upon it. This fact led me, as will be seen in the next chapter, to carbonize these juices, and also those of flowers and the grasses, by which means I procured the full extent of the ray action almost instantaneously. An alcoholic tincture of red peppers, properly carbonized, and spread upon paper, will give a picture in colors in one second. The impression is latent, and is promptly developed by immersion in warm ammonio-nitrate of silver, slightly perfumed with the essence of lavender, cassia, and cloves. Indeed, these experiments may be varied almost infinitely. For example, these vegetables contain glucose, or grape sugar. This, it is known, will reduce several salts to their metallic state. In the course of this reduction, the colorific principle of the particular vegetable employed may be supposed to modify the action so as to produce colors. So at least it turns out on actual experiment. Now, governed by this, in one sense assumed hypothesis, I would proceed in a given case as follows :

I would thoroughly soak a piece of paper with the juice of the vegetable, whose behavior, under light, comported with the behavior, under light, of the chemical agents I wished to combine with the vegetable constituents. Thus, the juice of the common carrot is bleached by light, and gives a yellow picture, on a white ground; the juice of strawberries is also bleached, and gives a red picture, on a white ground; the juice of violets is also bleached, and gives a blue picture on a white ground. Very good; now unite this combination with Mr. Hunt's hydriodate process, detailed in the preceding chapter, using the most colorific salt—hydriodate of baryta—and you have two bleaching processes united in one, and the result will be natural colors—depending, of course, for their strength and truthfulness on the degree of impregnation of your paper, and on certain niceties of manipulation. The operation is on the descending chromatic scale, and the degree of color obtained will never surpass the degree of impregnation. By alternately dipping and drying the paper a great number of times, your final result will be quite a strong picture. In the same manner, indicated above, you may unite these juices, whether of roots, fruit, flowers or grasses, with a great number of the metallic salts.

The above is written to give a general idea of the colorific properties of these vegetables, and of the manner of using them. Under the head of "Experiments" I have detailed a great number of processes for their use. I shall now dwell more at length on the character of these agents, with a special view to their chemical and heliochromic properties.

I—ESCULENT VEGETABLES, FRUITS, FLOWERS, AND GRASSES, CHEMICALLY CONSIDERED.

The inquiry into the cause of vegetable colors is most certainly a chemical one. The laws of chemistry hold sway over the molecular form of these coloring principles, governing this form, or structure, in an infinite variety of methods. These colors, in other words, have a definite chemical constitution. The well known law of chemistry, termed the law of definite proportions:—that is, that every compound body has a particular number of elements, and a definite number of each element—holds good in the case of vegetable colors. The true method of studying the nature and cause of vegetable colors, is by the ultimate analysis of vegetables themselves, in all the stages of their existence. Until this method was adopted, chemists could only conjecture and hypothecate. This led to many whimsical theories. One was, that the iron contained in vegetables was the cause of their color; but since the doctrines of direct analysis have obtained, it has been demonstrated that the quantity of iron in any vegetable is totally inadequate to produce the splendid colors which vegetation assumes.

Now, the principal elements of vegetable substances are oxygen, hydrogen, carbon, and a trace of nitrogen. The latter, according to Liebig, the great agricultural chemist, is always present, though in very minute quantity. There is also a variety of earthy substances in vegetables, such as lime, iron, magnesia, soda, potash, etc.; but all these never exist in one vegetable. The three elements, oxygen, hydrogen, and carbon, form from 95 to 99 per cent. of the entire vegetable. The great mass of all vegetables is composed of woody fibre, gum, starch, and sugar. The composition of these is as follows:

	Carbon.	Oxygen.	Hydrogen.
Woody fibre, . . .	15	10	10
Gum, ...	12	11	11
Starch, ...	12	10	10
Sugar, ...	12	11	11

Observe, in the above analysis, that the oxygen and hydrogen are in the same proportion as that in which they unite to form water. As a general rule, you will find all saccharine and mucilaginous vegetables will bear out the same proportions. But when you find a vegetable with the proportion of carbon below the above standard, it is oily or resinous. The subjoined analysis of vegetable substances shows this to be the case:—

	Carbon.	Hydrogen.	Oxygen.
Oil of Turpentine . .	10	8	0
Oil of Potatoes, . . .	5	6	1
Oil of Cloves, . . .	23	14	5
Gamboge, ...	20	14	5
Caoutchouc, ...	4	4	0
Beeswax, ...	37	39	2

Again, when the hydrogen is deficient, the vegetable generally has an acid character. Green fruit is eminently of this character—hence its deleterious effects when eaten. As the fruit ripens it assimilates more hydrogen, and becomes more saccharine. The following table will show the low rate of hydrogen in the principal vegetable acids:—

	Carbon.	Oxygen.	Hydrogen.
Acetic Acid, ...	4	3	3
Citric Acid, ...	4	4	2
Tartaric Acid, . . .	4	5	2
Gallic Acid, ...	7	5	3
Tannic Acid, . . .	18	12	8

In analyzing a vegetable we operate on the whole mass—its fibre, gum, starch, sugar, and coloring matter. So in the employment of its coloring matter for heliochromic purposes we cannot insulate it; that is, we cannot entirely detach it from its mixture with the organic constituents of the vegetable. Hence you will see the utility of the above tables. If, for example, you wish to employ the juice of the peel of peaches, or apples, or strawberries, you should bear in mind that they contain citric acid, which has a low equivalent of hydrogen; but they also contain sugar, with its high equivalent of hydrogen; and both of these substances have a large amount of carbon. Therefore, in operating with them you may safely employ oxydizing agents, but should guard against the too free use of carbon and hydrogen.

The above are general principles for the guidance of the amateur. They should be employed as we would use an arithmetical table; and by constantly bearing them in mind we will save ourselves many useless experiments, and a world of unnecessary trouble. I now pass to the consideration of

2. *The Heliochromic relations of these Agents.*

In Gilroy's "Treatise on Dyeing and Calico Printing," occurs a passage so much to the point in this place that I extract a great portion of it. This able writer comes so near to my own views, that I feel a special gratification in borrowing his language.

"Speaking of vegetable green, Berthollet says, 'the green of plants is undoubtedly produced by a homogeneous substance, in the same way as the greater number of hues which exist in nature. This color owes, then, its origin sometimes to simple rays, and sometimes to the union of different rays; and some other colors are in the same predicament. Were the green of plants due to two substances, one of which is yellow and the other blue, it would be extraordinary if we could not separate them, or at least change their proportions by some solvent.' The idea of Berthollet, that the green of plants is a distinct substance, existing in the plant, has been since verified. It is obtained by bruising green leaves into a pulp with water, pressing out all the liquid, and boiling the dry pulp in alcohol; when the alcohol is evaporated, there remains a deep green matter, which by digesting in water, dissolves, and frees it from a little brown coloring matter with which it was mixed. This substance has been named *chlorophyl.* The formation of chlorophyl seems to depend entirely upon the action of the solar rays. It is known that the function of the leaves and other green parts of plants is to absorb carbonic acid, and with the aid of light and moisture to appropriate its carbon. These processes are continually in operation: they commence with the formation of the leaves, and do not cease with their perfect development. But when light is absent, or, during the night, the decomposition of carbonic acid does not proceed; nay, carbonic acid is emitted, and oxygen gas absorbed; *it is evident then that a plant kept always excluded from the light must have a difference in its composition.* No one can have failed to observe the difference between vegetables thriving in the full enjoyment of light, and those which grow in obscure situations, or which are entirely deprived of its agency; the former are of brilliant tints, the latter dingy and white.

"From these facts we see that the green color of vegetables is owing to a peculiar approximate element existing in the vegetable, not invariably, nor altogether essential to the plant, but depending upon circumstances; these circumstances being at the same time the best for the health and existence of the plant. This color differs from the other colors of vegetables in the time of its appearing. Flowers of plants do not appear till the plant has reached a certain state of maturity; but whenever a plant rises above the soil, it immediately begins to assume the green hue, and this hue is continued till the object of the leaves is completed. When a chemical change takes place, the green passes away, and another color, reddish-yellow, takes its place. These changes are effected in different degrees, and in different lengths of time, just according as the leaves have the property of absorbing oxygen gas. Those leaves which continue longest green absorb oxygen slowest. The leaves of the holly will only absorb a small fraction of oxygen, in the same time that the leaves of the poplar and beech will absorb eight or nine times their bulk. These last are remarkable for the rapidity and ease with which the color of their leaves changes. That leaves do absorb oxygen gas when they change color at autumn, and that it is owing to the absorption of this gas, may be verified by placing some green leaves of the poplar, the beech, and the holly, under the receiver of an air-pump, and drying them thoroughly, keeping them excluded from light; when taken out, wet them with water, and place them immediately under a glass globe, full of oxygen gas, they will change color; and it will be found that each will change color just in proportion to the quantity of oxygen it absorbs. The consequence of this absorption is the formation of an acid. This acid changes the chlorophyllite, or green principle, from green to yellow, and then to a reddish hue. If we treat green leaves with an acid, the same changes of color take place, and if we macerate a red leaf in potash it becomes green.

"The various and beautiful colors of flowers are produced by a somewhat different process from that of the green of the leaves, in so far as they do not appear until the plant has attained a certain state of maturity. 'The leaves of the plant being fully developed, they take in more nourishment from the atmosphere than what is necessary for the existence of the plant. This extra nourishment takes a new direction; a peculiar transformation takes place; new compounds are formed, which furnish constituents of the blossoms, fruit, and seed.' *

"It is very probable that all the colors of flowers depend upon only a few approximate elements formed in the vegetable, in the manner already described, and that their various hues are the consequence of the presence of acids affecting more or less this coloring substance. This is the most probable hypothesis that has been formed, and with which we must rest satisfied till more accurate experiments verify its truth, or give us a better. The following summary of experiments will give some idea of the views held upon this subject:—'The expressed juice of most red flowers is blue; hence it is probable that the coloring matter in the flower is reddened by an acid, which makes its escape when the juice is exposed to the air. The violet is well known to be colored by a blue matter, which acids change to red; and alkalies and their carbonates, first to green, and then to yellow. The coloring matter of the violet exists in the petals of red clover, the red tips of the common daisy of the field, of the blue hyacinth, the hollyhock, lavender, in the inner leaves of the artichoke, and numerous other flowers. The same substance made red by an acid, colors the skins of several kinds of plums; probably, also, gives the red color to the petals of the scarlet geranium, and of the pomegranate tree. The leaves of the red cabbage, and the rind of the long radish, are also colored by this principle. It is remarkable that these, on being merely bruised, become blue, and give a blue infusion with water. It is probable that the reddening acid in these cases is the carbonic, which, on the rupture of the vessel which incloses it (being a gas), escapes into the atmosphere. If the petals of the red rose be triturated with a little water and chalk, a blue liquid is obtained. Alkalies render this blue liquid green, and acids restore its red color.'"

* Liebig's Agricultural Chemistry.

The identity of the coloring principle of flowers, with that of radish and red cabbage, referred to by Mr. Gilroy, I can verify from my experiments. The juice of flowers, and that of the cabbage and radish, have always comported alike, with similar treatment, under the influence of the colored rays of light. Carrots, beets, onions, squashes, pumpkins, watermelons, tomatoes, lettuce, asparagus, rhubarb, and sage, act differently, in union with re-agents; though I have no doubt that, in most respects, all the various colors, whether in vegetable or flower, depend upon a very similar origin, and are variegated by similar causes.

Our knowledge of this intricate subject is limited, of course; but I take great pleasure in recording my own mite of information. I have found, from experiment, that the blue matter which colors the violet is changed to red by acids, and first to green, and then to yellow by alkalies. The green at first formed results from the mixture of blue and yellow. Red rose leaves, when triturated with a little chalk and water, yield a blue liquor, which is rendered green by alkalies, and restored to red by acids. This is true, also, of most of the red flowers, such as the peony, dahlia, poppy, peach blows, sky rocket, lilac, and red-clover blows. The color of yellow flowers, I have observed, is generally more permanent than that of blue or red. It is usually, but not always, rendered paler by acids, and deeper by alkalies. That of the tiger lily, marigold, dandelion, nasturtium, daisies, and St. John's wort, is readily soluble in water, and in solution of potassa, communicating a brownish-yellow color; this is turned to cherry-red by the acids, to greenish-blue by carbonate of soda, and to yellow and red by several metallic salts. I have also found that most of the coloring matter of flowers is readily bleached by sulphurous acid. A paper prepared with a combination of different colors, will give a latent image, which is bleached in the ratio of the action of the different colored rays; and in this way weak sulphurous acid, or the vapor of burning sulphur, may be used as a developer. When the vegetable wash is followed by one of nitrate of silver, the picture may be developed by sulphuretted hydrogen, or by exposure over a tray of hydrosulphuret of ammonia.

As a general thing, the coloring matter of flowers may be extracted by macerating with dilute alcohol. It is better to use it at once; but it may be preserved with a little creosote, as already stated. The extract should be made and kept in total darkness. It should be applied to the paper, in a dark room, with the light of a candle only. Success is impossible, if the precautions are not observed.

The coloring matter of flowers which can be extracted by strong alcohol and ether, may be used in collodion, and in this menstruum it is acted upon more rapidly by the light. It may also be used in albumen, where water alone is employed to obtain the extract, or where you simply press out the juice. In this case you may dilute the white of eggs nearly one half with the vegetable juice, or infusion, and coat the glass, as with collodion. The film should be dried by a gentle heat. Then, if you wish to impregnate with other chemicals, you may do this by immersion. There are many other points of great interest connected with floral heliochromy, if I may use the term, but they will come more appropriately under the head of "experiments."

Thus far I have treated mostly of flowers. I need not dwell here particularly on the coloring matter of fruit. Suffice it to say, that this may be extracted and used in the same way as that of flowers. The peach, cherry, apple, strawberry, blackberry, raspberry, whortleberry, sumac bobs, currants, grapes, bittersweet, sun-flower seeds, pokeberries, elderberries, and squawberries, are the principal fruits upon which I have experimented. I will mention here, however, that I shall detail a great number of experiments with other vegetable coloring matter—such as cochineal, madder, annatto, gamboge, logwood, brazilwood, turmeric, golden seal, fustic, safflower, seed lac, gniacum, litmus, red sanders, and quercitron. Some of these experiments will be found to possess a surpassing interest; but the substances here referred to are too well known to require minute description.

I shall now pass to the consideration of the coloring matter of leaves and grasses; and what I have to offer here will be under three heads :—

1. *Chlorophyl.*—This is the substance from which leaves and the grasses derive their green color. It was first obtained in its pure state by Berzelius. It is procured by digesting leaves in renewed portions of ether. This tincture is then evaporated on a water-bath, and the deposit separated, dried, and treated with alcohol as long as green soluble matter is abstracted. The alcoholic solution is evaporated to dryness, and the residue digested in strong muriatic acid. The green acid solution is filtered, and mixed with water, by which the chlorophyl is precipitated; this precipitate is boiled in water, and afterwards dissolved in a strong solution of caustic potash, which is then diluted, filtered, and precipitated by acetic acid. The precipitate, washed and dried, is pure chlorophyl. In mass it is a dark green, but grass-green when reduced to powder. It is insoluble in water, but somewhat soluble in alcohol and ether. Alcohol, ether, and the essential oils dissolve it, when they are charged with a portion of potash. Pure potash and its carbonates dissolve it completely. A good way to fasten it upon paper is to wash the paper with the potash solution, and then soak the paper in a large quantity of solution of alum. This washes out the excess of potash, and strikes a fine green color; or you may soak a glass, coated with plain collodion, in the potash solution, and then in alum water; or you may evaporate the potash solution, and it will deposit chlorophyllate of potassa, which is soluble in water, with a fine green tint.

2. *Xanthophyl* is the coloring matter extracted from the yellow leaves of autumn. It is rapidly bleached by light, especially by the violet, blue, and red rays. I have obtained it as follows: Digest the leaves in a bottle, entirely filled with alcohol of sp. gr. 0·833, and well stopped, to exclude the air, else they will change from yellow to brown. Distil off most of the alcohol, and allow the residue to cool slowly, when the xanthophyl is

deposited, together with a little resinous and fatty matter. These impurities, I have found, are no detriment to its use in heliochromy. Xanthophyl is insoluble in water, and very sparingly soluble in alcohol and potash water, but readily dissolves in ether. An ethereal solution, therefore, may be used for either paper or collodion; indeed, I have found it very effective to simply bruise the leaves in ether, and to wash paper, nor change collodion with the filtered liquid. You will find a very curious experiment further on, in which I used neither paper or collodion, but a leaf itself, and produced a very good picture.

3. *Erythrophyl.*—All trees and shrubs, the leaves of which redden in autumn, bear red fruit. This is true of cherry, currant, mountain ash, sumac, and other trees and shrubs. This red coloring matter is obtained by digesting the red leaves in alcohol, and distilling the red tincture. It is purified by adding water to the residue, and filtering, to separate precipitated fat and resin. Solution of acetate of lead is then added to the clear filtrate as long as brown precipitate is formed, which is washed and decomposed by sulphuretted hydrogen. The sulphuret of lead formed is separated on a filter, and the filtrate evaporated to dryness: the erythrophyl remains in the form of a red extract. Its combinations with bases are of a grass-green color. Digested in alkalics, or their carbonates, the resulting solution is green; but acids reproduce the red color.

The alcoholic tincture first named may be used, without further preparation, in paper or collodion. The grass called red-top, mixed with clover leaves and blows, and ribbon-grass, and digested in alcohol a few days, gave me an extraordinary combination. It was used in paper, and the wet paper frozen between two plates of glass, by artificial means, simultaneously with the exposure of the paper in the camera. The exposure was but for a few seconds, and no picture was visible after the paper was withdrawn from the camera; but on submitting the paper to very weak sulphuretted hydrogen for about two hours, the picture was developed. The red, blue, yellow, violet, green, and russet were beautifully defined. Unfortunately, this picture faded out in a few days. I afterwards found that soaking one in a weak and perfectly neutral solution of nitrate of silver, for a few seconds, then, after a slight rinsing with water, immersing it for a moment in hyposulphate of soda, and rinsing copiously with water, the picture became fixed.

The leaves of the common pussy willow possess many remarkable qualities; an ethereal solution of them spread on paper, and exposed to actinic influence for a few seconds, is very curiously modified. If after the paper is withdrawn from the camera, and spontaneously dried, it is washed over with a solution of neutral chloride of gold, and then exposed over a jar containing an alcoholic or ethereal solution of phosphorus, the gold will not be reduced on the portions acted upon by the light, but is freely reduced on the other portions; thus giving a picture in which the lights are white paper and the shades gold. Impressions of fern and other leaves, and figured lace, obtained in this way by superposition, are very beautiful; and the process might, by such applications, be applied to purposes of ornament. The color of the ground may be varied at pleasure, by the simple act of dyeing. The leaves of the butternut tree act in a similar manner; those of sugar maple, peach, pear, plum, apple, beech, birch, ash, iron wood, walnut, and chestnut, will not produce this effect; but they each have other peculiarities.

I now come to the second general head of this chapter, viz.—

II.—ARTIFICIAL COLORIFIC AGENTS.

Under this head I shall include the metals (they being assayed by artificial means, and used in the arts), the salts of the metals, the acids, and the alkalies.

1. *The Metals.* The king of metals is gold; but as an actinic medium it is far inferior to some other metals. Alloyed with silver it assumes an importance which does not belong to it

in its purity. By melting together one part of gold and ten of silver, and rolling it into a plate, I obtained a surface which gave a peculiar richness to my Heliochromes. I arrived at the same result by amalgamating these proportions of the two metals with mercury, rubbing the amalgam on a copper plate, and driving off the mercury by heat. I have varied this method of forming plates, by adding one tenth of zinc. This I did by means of the electrotype process, that is, by precipitating on a copper plate the three metals from a mixture of their cyanides. I prefer these to any other plates. As they will be referred to hereafter, I will now designate them as the alloy plates.

Silver is the most important metal in its relations to light. This metal and its combinations, lie at the base of every valuable actinic process thus far discovered. That other beautiful and practical processes will yet be discovered in which silver, and, perhaps, all other metals will play no part, I do not doubt. Vegetable colors, the resins, and even animal products, contain the germs of many such a process. But I speak now of the present state of our science. As far as we know, nothing can replace this precious metal. For the reproduction of natural colors, no other substance, out of the great number I have tried, will bear comparison with silver. A plate of perfectly pure silver will give my Heliochromes in great perfection; but when it is alloyed with zinc and gold, as I have mentioned above, the tone of the pictures is improved, and the ray action is greatly accelerated. The following is a ready method of preparing an alloy plate. Polish a common daguerreotype plate, and rub it with a tuft of cotton dipped into dilute sulphuric acid, and then into an amalgam of one part gold and one part zinc, with the smallest practicable amount of mercury. Apply heat to drive off the mercury, and when the plate is cold, float its surface with a strong solution of bi-chromate of potash, slightly acidulated with oil of vitriol. This leaves the silver blanched, in which state it is readily polished; or it may be used without polishing, in which case the resulting picture will be without gloss.

For ordinary experiments, I have been in the habit of using the Scovill and the star plate. The former work best when galvanized. The copper in the Scovill plate is injurious ; but when galvanized, these plates are unequalled.

Copper, as a tablet for heliochromes, is possessed of some singular properties. Coated heavily with iodine, or, better still, chloride of iodine, and exposed to a colored image, in a camera box through which is diffused a weak vapor of sulphuretted hydrogen, it gives a sort of mongrel picture—part natural colors, and part iridescence. Copper alone, or alloyed, in the usual way, with silver, has given me no perfect results; but under certain treatment, detailed hereafter, it acts in a most interesting manner. Platina, deposited on silver, by the battery, in an exceedingly thin layer, affords a tablet of some interest. A thin plate of iron, or steel, highly polished, and thinly silvered, gives rise to another interesting process. Some peculiar uses of zinc, lead, antimony, arsenic, osmium, iridium, cobalt, selenium, mercury, tin, bismuth, nickel, potassium, sodium, and aluminum, will be detailed in a future chapter.

The alloys of some of the metals are worthy of special attention. "When we remember," says an able writer, "that out of eleven metals there are formed some thirty or more alloys, what may we not hope for when this subject shall have received its due attention at the hands of the chemist!" The following table of alloys will enable any ingenious person to form his own tablets for experimenting. A good Hessian crucible, and a charcoal furnace, with a pair of handbellows, will enable the amateur to form some interesting compounds. A plate of polished steel forms a very good mould, by means of which you may procure a fair surface. In making an alloy, you must melt the least fusible metal first. In the case of volatile metals, as mercury or zinc, the alloy may be formed by exposure to the fumes. For example, you may form a plate with a brass surface, by holding a copper plate over burning zinc; and this brass plate acts, heliochromically, as if it was a separate metal. So with gold or silver;—they may be amalgamated, with a powdery surface, by exposure to the vapor of mercury. This surface may be rendered bright by rubbing with a piece of buckskin.

The following are the principal alloys I have used in my experiments:

Copper.	Zinc.	Tin.	Lead.	Bismuth.	Nickel.	Brass.	Name of Alloy.
18	15						Tombac.
75	25						Prince's Metal.
50	25				25		German Silver.
85		14					Egyptian Sword.
66·5		33·5					Speculum Metal.
	50	50					Spurious Silver Leaf.
		19	31	50			Fusible Metal.
		75	9	8	Antimony. 8		Queen's Metal.

2. *The Salts of the Metals.*—First in the list, as the base of many operations, is nitrate of silver. It is made thus:—Dissolve silver coin in nitric acid, diluted with half water, by the aid of heat. Dilute plentifully with water, and stir in solution of common salt (chloride soda) till all the silver is precipitated in the form of a curdy white mass (chloride of silver); wash with water till the taste of salt and acid is gone; drain off all the water save enough to cover it, and add to this about one-fourth part sulphuric acid, and some lumps of zinc. The rule is to add enough acid to create a lively effervescence. Set it aside for twenty-four hours, or until the chloride is all reduced to a dark powder, which is metallic silver. Take out the pieces of zinc remaining, and add a little more sulphuric acid, and let it stand an hour. This will completely dissolve all the remaining particles of zinc. Wash thoroughly with water, and redissolve in nitric acid, dilute one half with water as before. Filter and evaporate to crystallization. Drain the crystals, and spread them on paper to dry. This is pure nitrate of silver, if the process has been properly managed. If it is not pure white, or does not give a clear solution in water, redissolve in water, filter, and again crystallize.

These crystals are soluble in one part cold, in half a part boiling water, in four parts boiling alcohol, insoluble in pure nitric acid. Nitrate of silver fuses readily, and congeals to a white fibrous mass. It does not blacken by light, unless organic matter be present. United to almost any vegetable or animal matter, it is readily acted upon by light. Even the bony substances, as ivory, horn, gum, &c., give it this property. A tablet of wood, in this respect, forms a photographic material. You can take a picture on your own skin, or finger nail, by soaking the part in warm solution of a chloride, as common salt, for half an hour, wiping off the liquid, and holding the part in ammonio-nitrate of silver for a few minutes in the dark. Then fasten on the part a transparent engraving, by means of pasting the corners, and be around in the light. Fix in hyposulphate of soda, and rinse with water.

Chloride of Silver is formed by mingling solutions of the nitrate and chloride of soda (common salt), or any other chloride, or hydrochloric acid. It is cleansed from acid and salt by washing in water. Chloride of silver, when pure, is beautifully white, but darkens rapidly in the light. Under the red ray it is tinted red. By the other rays it is blackened, and converted into sub-chloride of silver. It may also be reduced to sub-chloride by the action of chlorides of copper and mercury and per-chloride of iron, and may be formed directly by the action of muriatic acid and sub-oxide of silver. Sub-chloride of silver is a brownish or black powder. It is an important agent in heliochromy. The white chloride fuses at 500° to a clear yellow liquid. It congeals to a transparent, colorless solid, so soft as to receive the impression of the finger nail. In this fact lies a beautiful process, for the first preparation of heliochromic tablets.

Iodide and *Bromide* of silver are formed by mutual decomposition, like the chloride. Iodide or bromide of potassium are the salts generally used to mingle with the nitrate. These salts both fuse to a red liquid, and congeal to a yellow mass. They are useful, but not essential, in my collodiochrome.

Fluoride of Silver is formed by the action of hydrofluoric acid on carbonate of silver. When dry it is fusible, like the chloride. It is soluble in water, and mingles freely with the other silver salts, in which way I make use of it.

Ammonio-nitrate, or *Ammoniuret of Silver*, is formed by adding aqua ammoniæ to solution of nitrate of silver, until the precipitate at first formed is exactly re-dissolved. A little nitrate solution should then be added, to prevent the least excess of ammonia. Or, you may dissolve nitrate of silver in aqua ammoniæ, and obtain ammoniuret in crystals.

Fulminate of Silver.—This very singular and dangerous compound is prepared as follows: 100 grains of fused and finely powdered nitrate of silver are added to 1 oz. warm alcohol, and the mixture stirred in a large basin. An ounce of fuming nitric acid is then added. A violent effervescence follows, and a white powder falls. Cold water is added, and the powder is immediately collected on a filter, and dried at 100°. The contact of a hard body causes this substance to explode with great violence. It is unsafe to make more than the product of a sixpence at once, though I once made a half dollar into this fulminate, and had the pleasure of standing within three feet of it when it exploded. As a wonder of mercy, I escaped unhurt; but if the reader doubts my assertion that it made somewhat of a racket, let him try the experiment. I was deaf as an adder for a week.

Citrate of Silver.—This is formed by adding a citrate, as citrate of soda, to a soluble salt of silver, as the nitrate. It is a brilliant white powder. Paper, or collodion, impregnated with a citrate, and then dipped into nitrate of silver, will furnish the citrate of silver in a form for experimenting. Joined with iron, in the form of ammonio-citrate of iron, it affords a curious actinic agent.

Silvate of Silver.—This important salt is made thus:—Mix alcoholic solutions of nitrate of silver and silvic acid, and add ammonia. A white precipitate falls, which must be caught on a filter. It is soluble in ether.

The *Cyanide, Hyposulphite, Carbonate, Phosphate, Borate, Chromate,* and *Aluminate of Silver* are formed by mutual decomposition, by means of mingling solutions of cyanide, hyposulphite, &c., of potassa or soda with nitrate of silver. Some of these salts will be referred to again.

I shall now pass to the consideration of some of the Salts of Gold. Those of zinc, lead, iridium, cobalt, &c., will receive all necessary attention in a more appropriate place.

Chloride of Gold, in great purity, is made thus :—Dissolve gold coin in nitro-muriatic acid, by the aid of a water-bath heat. The acid should be made by mixing one part nitric, and two parts muriatic acids. Dilute the solution with about four parts water, and stir into it an excess of strong, well-filtered solution of sulphate of iron. Let it stand twenty-four hours, when all the gold in the coin will be precipitated as a dark chocolate-colored powder. Wash this several times in water, and re-dissolve in the smallest possible quantity of nitro-muriatic acid. Evaporate over a water-bath until the chloride, on cooling, will concrete into a waxy mass. Bottle immediately, as it is very deliquescent in the air.

Hyposulphite of Gold, or *Sel d'Or.*—I have a very neat process for making this beautiful salt. It is this.—Dissolve one part chloride of gold in the smallest possible amount of water, and filter. Dissolve three parts hyposulphite of soda in the least possible quantity of water. Add the gold to the soda solution, drop by drop, with constant agitation, and let the mixture stand until it will filter clear. Add this to five or six times its bulk of ninety-five per cent. alcohol—shake, and let it stand a few hours—when the sel d'or will be precipitated as fine brilliant needles. Throw into a filter, catch and dry the crystals. I have given this process in detail, on account of the importance of this salt in heliochromy.

Iodide of Gold.—Add solution of chloride of gold to solution of iodide of potassium till a dark green precipitate forms, and until this precipitate becomes permanent, for the first portion formed is re-dissolved on agitation. It is soluble in hydriodic acid, in which state I use it.

Bromide of Gold.—Dissolve gold leaf in pure bromine. On evaporation it leaves a dark grey mass, soluble in water, from which it may be obtained in dark red crystals. This salt is so intense a color, that it gives a tinge to 5,000 parts of water.

Chloride of Gold, and *Hydrofluoric Acid*, or *Fluoride of Potassium*, form a mixture, which, added to other compounds, holds an important place in some of my processes.

The Purple of Cassius.—When protochloride of tin is added to a dilute solution of chloride of gold, a dirty purple precipitate is formed, which is purple of Cassius, so called after the name of the chemist who discovered it. A better colored precipitate is formed when the protochloride of tin is added to a solution of perchloride of iron till the color of the liquid has a shade of green, and adding this liquid drop by drop, to a solution of perchloride of gold, very dilute; after twenty-four hours a brown powder is deposited which is slightly transparent and purple red by transmitted light. When dried and powdered it is a dull blue color. This powder is used in porcelain painting, and for tinging glass of a fine red color.

Cyanide of Gold.—Dissolve from fifty to one hundred grains chloride of gold in one pint of water. Dissolve one ounce cyanide of potassium in a little water, and add this, with stirring, to the gold solution. Or you may dissolve one ounce cyanide in a little water, saturate it with chloride of gold, and then add a small lump of cyanide to insure an excess. Dilute this to one pint. I use this in many ways. For gilding with it attach to the article to be gilt a piece of bright zinc, of nearly its size, and immerse both in the solution. Two or three drops of bi-sulphuret of carbon added to the above solution cause the gold to be deposited in a more brilliant form. This is also a valuable addition to cyanide of silver.

Sulpho-cyanide of Gold is a flesh-colored powder, which falls when solution of sulpho-cyanide of potassium is mixed with chloride of gold. It is soluble in the precipitant, and in ammonia.

Polychrome Gold.—I have coined this name as expressive of a union of polychrome with gold. Polychrome I prepare very readily as follows :—I digest horse-chestnut-bark in alcohol for two or three days, concentrate the liquor to the consistence of a syrup by distillation in a common retort, and set this aside for some weeks to crystallize. These crystals I wash with ice-water, to free them from extractive matter, and dissolve them in a boiling mixture of five parts ninety-five per cent. alcohol with one of sulphuric ether, from which, by cooling, the polychrome separates, perfectly colorless, and usually as a light powder, like magnesia alba. It dissolves in 672 parts of water at 50°, and in 13 parts at 212°. The solution is colorless by transmitted, but slightly blue by reflected light; acids destroy this property, but it is restored by a few drops of any alkali. It does not precipitate any of the metallic salts; but its mixture with salts of gold has extraordinary properties. The powder dissolves abundantly in alkaline liquors, and the solutions give a magnificent play of colors with reflected light. In a reflected spectrum they are perfectly gorgeous and dazzling. The polychrome-gold I prepare by neutralizing sel d'or with a very little carbonate of potash, and adding it (fifty grains of sel d'or) to four ounces solution of polychrome, containing one hundred grains polychrome and one drachm liquid ammonia. I keep this in a bottle perfectly covered with black paint, and never open it to the daylight.

Protochloride of Tin, so much used as a mordant in dyeing, is obtained by dissolving tin in strong muriatic acid until it is saturated, and evaporating. The salt crystallizes in long prisms. They are soluble in water; for a very dilute solution a few drops of muriatic acid should be added to the water, else it is decomposed into a basic salt.

The *Nitrate, Sulphate,* and *Chloride of Copper,* can be cheaply purchased, of a pure quality, from a chemist. So with the salts of lead, bismuth, iron, zinc, &c.; and I recommend this method of obtaining the limited quantity required by the subsequent processes.

III.—THE ACIDS.

These should be purchased of a pure quality. The principal acids I employ are the nitric, sulphuric, sulphurous, hydrochloric, hydrofluoric, citric, boracic, iodic, bromic, tartaric, uric, gallic, pyro-gallic, nitrous, acetic, and oxalic. A few of these agents which it is difficult to purchase pure, and which must be made in a certain way, I will notice in detail.

1. *Chloracetic Acid.*—Introduce into bottles about full of dry chlorine, a small quantity of concentrated acetic acid, and expose to direct sunshine. On hot days explosion sometimes occurs, but never immediately on exposure. The best way is to expose the bottles at a safe distance, and not to meddle with them until the next morning, when the chlorine will be gone, and the interior of the bottles lined with a crystalline deposit, consisting chiefly of chloracetic acid. Pour in each bottle a small quantity of water, which will give a strong chloracetic solution. Collect these into one bottle, and expose it in vacuo by the side of a vessel containing pieces of caustic potash and another containing sulphuric acid. The oxalic acid in the solution will first crystallize, and then the chloracetic acid, in rhombohedric crystals. Place these crystals on bibulous paper, which will partially free them from adhering acetic acid. The vapor of this acid is dangerously irritating. Boil a solution of this salt with excess of potassa, and the liquor deposits, on cooling, an abundant crop of crystals of chloride of potassium, and the mother liquor acts powerfully upon a solution of nitrate of silver, reducing it to the metallic state.

2. *Uric Acid.*—This is extracted from guano, and is found in the excrements of the parrot, the silkworm, and the boa-constrictor. It is readily extracted from the latter as follows :—Dry the excrements, reduce to powder, boil, first in alcohol, then in water : then digest in dilute hydrochloric acid, wash in water, and digest in

a hot solution of caustic potassa, filter, concentrate, press out the resulting pasty mass, and wash with water. Dissolve this in boiling water, and pour the hot solution into hydrochloric acid, when a white gelatinous precipitate falls, which is to be washed and dried. This is pure uric acid. Dissolve this in a weak solution of potassa, and evaporate, and urate of potassa separates as a dense crystalline powder. Slightly acidulate solution of this salt, and mix an excess with solution of nitrate of silver; urate of silver is the result, which blackens with a little heat.

3. *Chlorochromic Acid.*—Melt in a crucible a mixture of ten parts of common salt, and seventeen parts of bi-chromate of potash. Pour the melted mass on a slab to cool, break into small pieces, and fill a tubulated retort with the same. After attaching condensing receiver, pour forty parts of sulphuric acid on the mass. In a few minutes all the product distils over without the aid of heat. This singular acid is a blood red liquid, and fumes on exposure to the air; its vapor is red.

4. *Hydrofluoric Acid.*—This acid it is better to buy than to make. It comes in lead bottles; it is a dangerous poison, and should never be opened in a close room. I came near losing my life by working over the fumes of this acid. It produced bleeding at the lungs, and an entire prostration of my nervous system, accompanied by neuralgic pains of great severity. My whole system became charged with it; as a remedy I took minute doses of nitrate of silver, often repeated, with a view to the formation of fluoride of silver. The importance of this acid in heliochromy cannot be overrated.

IV.—THE ALKALIES.

Potash, soda, ammonia, baryta, lime, and strontia, and some of their salts, will occupy our attention in the present section. Ammonia is the volatile alkali; potash and soda the fixed alkalies; and lime, baryta, and strontia, the alkaline earths. Caustic potash and soda, and their carbonates, are indispensable. Those alkaline salts which are useful in heliochromy, I will notice in detail.

1. *Iodide of Potash.*—Dissolve iodine in potash solution, until the latter is completely neutralized. Evaporate to dryness, and heat the mass to redness, keeping it so as long as bubbles of oxygen gas are liberated. The residual mass is iodide of potash. Let it get cold, and dissolve it in its weight of boiling water. Let it crystallize very slowly. This salt is convenient for forming other iodides.

2. *Bromide of Potash,* prepared exactly as the above, with the exception of substituting bromine for iodine. If before the fusion of either of these salts, a little charcoal is added, the result is better, as it entirely frees them from iodates.

3. *Fluoride of Potassium* is formed by saturating hydrofluoric acid with the potash, and evaporating to dryness. This salt bears an intense heat without change.

Iodide, bromide, and fluoride of silver and of other metals, are formed with these salts by mutual decomposition. The solution of fluoride of potash corrodes glass. It is decomposed by chlorine. A solution of a chloride with this fluoride, will give fluorine, in a nascent state, on the immersion of a plate of silver. All three of these salts are soluble in water; but slightly so in alcohol. On addition of sulphuric acid to their solutions, they evolve their respective vapors.

4. *Nitrate of Potash.* Nitre. Saltpetre.—This salt is an abundant natural product, lixiviated from certain soils in the East Indies. In France and Germany it is artificially produced in what are termed nitre beds. Nitre, to be fit for photographic use, should be refined, which is done by recrystallizing; and always while it is recrystallizing it should be stirred, so that the crystals may be small. The crystals should then be washed and completely dried. It should also be dried again after pulverizing, before it is used for making gun cotton, as even a little water may create an undue heat, on the addition of the sulphuric acid. This should never be neglected.

5. *Cyanide of Potash.*—Formed by saturating a concentrated solution of caustic potash with hydrocyanic acid. It is a deadly poison; and should be purchased by the amateur, and used with care. For electrotyping, and as a fixing agent in the collodion process, it is invaluable. It is abundantly soluble in water. An electrotype solution of excellent quality may be formed by saturating a given quantity of water with cyanide of potash, and saturating this solution with chloride of silver, and then adding a little cyanide to give an excess. This solution is to be diluted with water to the working point.

6. *Chromate and Bi-chromate of Potash.*—Both these salts are extensively used in calico printing; and in connexion with the salts of lead, &c., produce some very brilliant tints. A paper washed with a mixture of two drachms saturated solution of the bi-chromate, and a solution of two drachms of sulphate of iron in ounce of water, exposed under a super-imposed engraving for from five to twenty minutes in strong sunshine, and then washed with a solution of nitrate of silver, gives a yellow picture. The picture shows faintly on coming from the frame; and if parts of it are then touched with a solution of ferro-cyanide of iron, these will be blue. By touching parts of the picture with solution of nitrate of silver of different strengths, you can obtain a range of colors from a bright yellow to a strong orange red. After the picture is fixed by soaking it in water, it may be rendered transparent by rubbing it with Dammar varnish, and other (oil) colors put on the back, with pleasing effect.

7. *Hyposulphite of Soda.*—This salt is now extensively manufactured in great purity. It is too well known among photographers to require description. It is an essential article in my processes.

8. *Chlorite of Soda.* Labarraque's liquid.—Prepared by passing the chlorine from 9 lbs. common salt, 7 lbs. manganese, 9 lbs. oil of vitriol, 7 lbs. water, into a solution 39 lbs. cryst. soda in 19½ galls. water. Or decompose a solution of chloride of lime by a solution of carbonate of soda, as long as carbonate of

lime precipitates, and add a little excess of alkali. This is a bleaching liquid.

9. *Biborate of Soda.* Borax.—Before using the borax of commerce, it should be dissolved in water, filtered, and evaporated to crystallization.

10. *Iodide of Baryta.*—Add a saturated alcoholic solution of iodine to a solution of proto-sulphuret of barium, as long as any sulphur separates, filter, evaporate almost to dryness, re-dissolve in a small portion of water, and boil it down in a flask to dryness. This salt has very singular colorific properties.

11. *Chloride of Lime.*—A good article of this salt can be purchased at the drug stores. It may be employed for several purposes in picture-making. A saturated solution in water, well settled and decanted, or filtered, may be used for mutual decomposition, for forming various metallic chlorides. Or the same solution may be made to give out chlorine gas, by adding sulphuric acid to it. In this way very exact quantities of the gas may be evolved, by simply regulating the amount of acid, and by dilution. To rid a room of sulphuretted hydrogen, and many other noxious gases, it may be used as above.

12. *Chloride of Strontia.*—Procurable in purity only from chemists. Soluble in water and alcohol. It imparts a brilliant-red color to alcohol flame.

V.—THE GASES AND VAPORS.

1. *Chlorine.*—Mix one part binoxide of manganese with two to three parts of concentrated hydrochloric acid, in a retort, and apply a gentle heat. Chlorine gas is abundantly evolved. By using a bent tube, and having the bent end reach nearly to the bottom of a bottle, the bottle will fill with the gas, by the displacement of the air. Or, you may conduct the gas into water, and thus form chlorine water. Chlorine is a yellowish green gas, of an astringent taste, and a suffocating odor. Even when diluted

with air, it excites spasm and irritation of the glottis. This gas has a strong affinity for hydrogen, uniting with it explosively, in sunshine. It unites readily with several metallic surfaces, especially silver, but it is difficult to procure as good a coating as with iodine. As it works better in presence of moisture, I succeeded in procuring beautiful coatings by first thinly covering the plate with a moist substance, as glue, honey, molasses, &c., and, after the coating forms, washing away this layer. A more ready method of chloridizing a silver plate is to immerse it in a chloride. Chloride of iron, formed by dissolving red oxyde of iron (rouge) in muriatic acid, gives a beautiful coating to a silver plate. Sulphate of copper dissolved in water, and the solution charged with muriatic acid, will do the same. Paper imbued with solution of nitrate of silver, and exposed to chlorine gas, may be charged with chloride of silver.

2. *Hydrogen.*—A convenient way to procure this gas is to place in a flask some sulphuric acid diluted with four parts of water, and add pieces of zinc. By attaching a tube to the flask you may collect the gas in a bell-glass over water. It may be employed in the camera, between the plate and lens, by simply placing some dilute sulphuric acid and zinc in a small bottle, and placing the bottle uncorked in the camera box. When it is required for developing, or reduction, a tight wooden box or a common coating jar answers well, always observing the precaution to interpose a muslin screen between the bottom of the jar and the plate, to prevent the water carried up by the gas from spattering the plate. Other gases may be used in the same way.

3. *Sulphuretted Hydrogen.*—Obtained by acting on sulphuret of antimony—one part—by muriatic acid—four parts—by the aid of heat. It is more conveniently made by acting on sulphuret of iron by dilute sulphuric acid. To purify it, pass it through an intermediate bottle of water at 80°, or through salt water. It is a gas of very unpleasant odor. Whoever has been to Sharon Springs, or, what is equivalent, had his nose in the neighborhood of rotten eggs, knows all about the smell of

this abominably fetid gas. A paper dipped in solution of nitrate of silver becomes beautifully iridescent on exposure to this gas; the silver is reduced to the metallic state. An argento-collodion, or albumen coating, is still more beautifully affected. The gas may be used in its nascent state, by simply immersing the article to be acted upon in the liquid where the gas is forming. Chlorine is a disinfectant of this gas.

4. *Selenium.*—This metal is extracted, by a lengthy process, from the reddish deposit formed in the manufacture of oil of vitriol from iron pyrites. It liquifies a little above 212°, and boils below a red heat, giving a darker yellow gas than chlorine.

5. *Sulphur.*—At 822° this well known substance boils and rises in a dark orange-colored vapor, which deposits flowers of sulphur on a cold body. By dipping pith, or other porous and inflammable bodies into melted sulphur, and setting fire to it, you may coat a glass or other surface with a layer of sulphur, and this surface, after iodizing or bromidizing, will give a picture which developes itself in the dark.

6. *Phosphorus.*—A convenient way to use the vapor of this singular substance, is to dissolve some of it in ether or alcohol, and place the solution in a coating jar. The plate, paper, or collodionized glass to be acted upon may be placed over it. In this way gold and silver may be reduced from their solutions to the metallic state. A fine coat of gold may thus be given to paper, leaves, laces, and other ornamented articles. The article must first be impregnated, or covered, with a solution of chloride of gold, of moderate strength, 10 grs. to the oz. of water. Gum water may be used for dissolving the chloride, where the article will only admit of a wash.

7. *Phosphuretted Hydrogen.*—Heat phosphorus in a solution of potash in dilute alcohol. It may be caught over mercury, or over boiled salt water. There are many other methods of making it; but the above simple method is the one I prefer, as the gas thus made is but little explosive. Its uses will be detailed hereafter.

8. *Oxygen.*—Heat chlorate of potash in a glass retort. It

gives off all its oxygen. A portion of peroxide of manganese, or of oxyde of copper, facilitates the reaction. In small quantities, and for immediate use, it may be collected in the pneumatic trough, in bell-glasses. This gas has a much greater influence in photographic operations than most persons imagine.

9. *Nitrous Oxyde.*—Heat nitrate of ammonia in a retort, and a colorless, inodorous gas is evolved, which induces intoxication when inhaled, and hence called " laughing gas."

10. *Nitric Oxyde.*—Generated by acting on copper filings by nitric acid. On mixing with air it becomes red. It gives a splendid coating to a plate of silver. The effects of light upon it are singular in the extreme.

11. *Hyponitric Acid Vapor.*—This vapor is deep red. The acid is prepared by the dry distillation of nitrate of lead, powdered and thoroughly desiccated.

12. *Iodine and Bromine* give off their vapors at common temperatures. That of the former is violet; that of the latter red. A gentle heat disengages them in great abundance.

CHAPTER VII.

EXPERIMENTS ON THE DAGUERREOTYPE PLATE.

Colors produced on the rotative principle.—The iodized, bromo-iodized, and chloro-iodized plate, each give these colors.—Mercury, at various temperatures—impinging at angles--alloyed.—The electrotyped, blanched, oxydized, grained, and greased plate.—New Developers.—Vapors of Zinc, Tin, Bismuth, Antimony, Arsenic, Molybdenum, Gold, Silver, Copper, Platina, Iridium, and Iron.—The Oxy-hydrogen Blowpipe.—Eliopole Lamp.—Voltaic flame.—Screens of Platina Gauze.—The Gases—Sulphuric, Nitric, Phosphuretted Hydrogen, Sulphuretted Hydrogen, Hydrogen, &c —The reversed Daguerreotype process.—Undercoatings, with Bromine, Chlorine, Per-fluoride of Chrome, Chlorochromic Acid, Carbonaceous Glaze.—Iodized Mercury Surface, developed with the vapor of Silver.—Colored Light for Developing.

It may not be known to the generality of my readers that a common Daguerreotype, or iodized silver plate, may be impressed with the solar spectrum ; but the fact has been tested by several experimentalists. Robert Hunt attributes the effect to iridescence. In other words, he accounts for it on the principle of Newton's rings. The colors, he contends, are produced by the infinitesimal and relative tenuity of the coating, as produced by the relative intensity of the action of the different colored rays of light. As shown in another chapter, this effect is not produced on the iodized plate, except on the principle of rotation ; that is to say, at one period of the exposure what should be green will be yellow, the yellow will presently be blue, and the blue will at length come to green. Hence, if you can watch close enough to catch the effect at the right time, you will have the colors properly located.

The fact, however, is an interesting one; and it led me into many experiments. These I will endeavor to describe as correctly and concisely as possible.

Experiment 1.—Iodize a plate to a bright cherry, or violet, superpose a colored print, or place it in the Camera, focussed on a colored object. The effect is as stated above; but it requires several hours of bright sunshine.

Experiment 2.—Iodize the plate as above. Then, before exposure to light, place it in chlorine gas, until it blackens. This plate under white light very speedily whitens. Exposed as in Ex. 1, it is affected like the iodized plate.

Experiment 3.—After iodizing the plate, bromidize it, as for a Daguerreotype, and repeat the experiment as in No. 1. The action of light is thus much accelerated and the effect as to coloration the same as above, only there is greater harmony, and the impression is more soft and silky.

Experiment 4.—Remove a plate, prepared by either of the above methods, from the light, at any period of its exposure, and place it over the mercury box, and the result is a picture in light and shade. I tried the mercury at many different temperatures, and the result was invariably light and shade. I also tried exposing the plate to the mercury at different angles; but the effect was the same. I thought it possible that the molecules of mercury might be induced to attach themselves, by impinging on the plate at an angle, in some peculiar manner productive of the desired phenomena. Alas! these experiments failed by the hundred. I can imagine no form of these experiments but what I tried. I used the mercury at a low temperature, and from that up to the boiling point; I tried large and small quantities, from a pound down to the smallest globule; I alloyed it with other metals; I even tried immersing the plate in cold, warm, and hot mercury; I tried rubbing the mercury on the plate; and I tried rubbing very many alloys of mercury, such as gold, silver, copper, lead, tin, bismuth, platina, iridium, zinc, &c., and that, too, in various proportions, but all to no purpose. Then I varied the condition of the silver surface, by blanching it, electrotyping it to a blue and a white, oxydizing it, roughening, or graining it, amalgamating it, greasing it, &c.; and, though the results were often quite curious and surprising, the colors would not come.

Experiment 5.—After working and twisting the above idea until my brain felt like India rubber, I struck off on a new track. Determined to get the colors from the iodized or bromo-iodized plate, it occurred to me to try new developers. The vapors of various metals were tried first. The more volatile metals, as zinc, lead, tin, bismuth, antimony, molybdenum, &c., were first in the crucible. The yellow tint of bismuth gave a sort of flesh color to the whites; but beyond this, and some peculiar effects of lead, I met with entire failure. By my carelessness in using the vapor of boiling arsenic I jeopardized my life. Then came the more refractory metals, such as gold, silver, copper, platina, and iron. How to vaporize them was the question. I tried the oxy-hydrogen blowpipe, the eliopole lamp, and finally succeeded with the voltaic blaze, produced by 100 pairs of galvanic batteries. These, and similar contrivances, I made myself, right here among the mountains, with no mechanics to aid me but a blacksmith and a house-carpenter. By both of these lights I took pictures, and I took them quickly; but after all, these luminaries are not like the strong, full, diffuse light of the sun. My method of using the vapor of these metals was to support the plate at such a distance above the heat that the latter would not injure the chemical coating. Here I met with a serious difficulty. The light of both these intense flames destroyed the effect of light in the camera. To remedy this, I interposed a veil of yellow or black cloth, which would intercept the light, and at the same time admit the passage of the metallic vapor. Out of this plan grew another difficulty:—the cloths would burn up. To remedy this, I tried to make them fire-proof, by various means, such as repeated soakings in alum-water. At length I found that three or four screens of platina wire gauze, placed about half an inch apart, answered the purpose perfectly. I placed the first gauze screen about four inches above the focus of the blaze. This became red-hot, but the succeeding ones were not so, and the arrangement answered well when the relative distances were kept up; for, otherwise, the vapor would condense upon the gauze.

The above course of experiments cost me six months hard labor. No colors were obtained; but it will be seen further on, that it was not lost labor.

Experiment 6.—I next tried the gases, and first of all, oxydizing agents, such as those of sulphuric and nitric acid. These gave no picture. I then had recourse to phosphuretted hydrogen. This would develope the picture in all the glory of iridescence. It would glow in all the colors of the rainbow; but the witching hues were not in place. I would often soliloquize, just to keep my courage up, by way of a little pleasantry:—"Oh, you naughty red, you sky-born blue, you green-as-grass green, you refractory yellow—why must you always be after getting into the wrong places! If I could teach you to know your places, it would be a fine lesson for all of ye; but instead thereof ye delight in getting as far from the mark as possible." Even while thus amusing myself, and taming my own impatience, these colors, like fairies in a dance, would change, and interchange places, in the face of my remonstrances, and in the very light where I held them. Well, well, thought I, the gem I seek after is somewhere in this crowd of wonders. So I would repeat the experiment in many varied forms; and I would obtain results truly marvellous, and very encouraging—when, lo!—away goes my apparatus—blown up, not sky-high, but slam-bang against the whitewashed wall, and every hair of my head pointing towards the wreck. Then I tried the less explosive kind of this gas; but this did not work so well; besides that, too, will sometimes explode, when you little dream of it. After a long time, I reluctantly gave up these thrilling experiments—not altogether because the gas was dangerous, but I began to get new light, in respect to the true nature of chemical re-actions, and fixed my mind and my hopes on other agents.

Experiment 7.—Still pursuing the gas idea, I next tried

developing with common hydrogen. The results were similar, but far less beautiful than those with phosphuretted hydrogen. Sulphuretted hydrogen succeeded well, but though, like its neighbor, the phosphuret, it would give a play of colors, I could not work the process into the natural colors. The idea of the simultaneous action of a gas with the light, was easily executed by generating the gas in the camera, or conducting it into the camera, while the plate was being exposed to light. With a plate coated to a green with chloride of iodine, and thus exposed to a very dilute gas (sulphuretted hydrogen), I obtained very fair reds and blues several times, in their proper localities. It required an exposure of several hours. Thus I went through the entire range of gases. It cost much time and money, and was seriously detrimental to health.

Experiment 8.—The idea of giving the iodide of silver an undercoating, occurred to me. I tried a reversed daguerreotype coating—the bromine first, and then the iodine; the chlorine first, and then the iodine. Then came bromine alone, and chlorine alone. I next undercoated with fluorine, per-fluoride of chrome, chlorochromic acid gas, &c. I pre-coated the plate with a sort of carbonaceous glaze, which I produced by greasing, and then strongly heating the plate; and this surface I exposed to iodine, bromine, and chlorine. Undercoating with mercury, and exceedingly slight deposits of gold, copper, and other metals, was also tried. All and each of these and other variations of the idea, were tried in connexion with the developers before named, but no colors appeared. The reader may think this was discouraging, but it was not; for the many curious, and often beautiful, results I obtained, were props to my hopes, and spurs to my industry. While thus reversing the order of the daguerreotype coatings, it occurred to me to reverse the entire process. So, I faced a silver plate with mercury, by rubbing a heavy coating of mercury on it. This I iodized, &c., and tried to develope colors over the vapor of silver, as obtained by the voltaic flame.

I could produce no picture. Then I tried the same process, with mercury for a developer, but with no better success.

Experiment 9.—All the above coatings I tried with colored light for a developer. Becquerel discovered that yellow and red light would develope the daguerrean image. I used yellow, red, green, and orange colored glasses; and some of the results were magically beautiful:—but—oh! that *but*—the images formed were mostly identical with the daguerreotype, but often more delicate, and of various peculiarities of tone.

In these, and many other experiments with the daguerreotype plate, I utterly failed of my object. I am now fully convinced that there are no colors in the process, excepting those which are due to the principle of iridescence, or to oxydation.

CHAPTER VIII.

EXPERIMENTS WITH VARIOUS METALS.

Tin, iodized and chloridated.—Copper, iodized, and colors developed with a gas.—Pictures in colors on Brass.—Singular behavior of Brass to the vapor of Mercury.—Lead.—Its iodide rendered heliochromic.—Iron and Steel, their extraordinary colorific susceptibility.—Zinc, employment of its vapor.—Nickel, Bismuth, and Antimony.—German Silver, Prince's Metal, and Britannia.—Thrilling experiments with their alloys.—The Alloy Plate.—Vapor of Arsenic.—Iridium.

EXPERIMENT 1.—I first tried tin. This I cut out of a new tin pan, and polished. It requires heat to coat this metal with iodine. By heating the tin plate in a close tin or earthen jar, with a little iodine inclosed, I obtained a brownish-red coating, sensitive to light, but not susceptible of coloration. A chloridated tin-surface is more sensitive than the above; and I had great hopes of this, from the fact of the chloride of tin being a mordant. After repeating the whole round of experimentation, I was again doomed to failure.

EXPERIMENT 2.—*Copper.* I coated a well polished copper plate with iodine, exposed it to a colored image, and developed a colored picture, with sulphuretted hydrogen. Some of the colors were properly located; but this, as I afterwards found, after many hundred experiments, was due to chance. Oxydation and iridescence constitute the whole of this process. A very slight amalgamation of the surface of the copper, with a weak solution of nitrate of mercury, heightened the effect.

EXPERIMENT 3.—*Brass.* An iodized surface of brass is sensitive to light; but the parts on which the light acts are not acted upon by mercury—the very reverse of the daguerreotype pl te. Hence a picture on brass has its shadows white, and its lights yellow. The gases, particularly the sulphuretted hydrogen, develope a picture somewhat like that on copper, as described in Ex. 2. A brass plate made by holding a plate of copper over burning zinc, is far the most sensitive.

EXPERIMENT 4.—*Lead.* I polished a tablet of sheet lead, and iodized it, in the usual way, to a deep yellow. I then exposed it to chlorine, until it assumed a blue. This plate gave a mingling of natural colors and iridescence.

EXPERIMENT 5.—*Iron and Steel,* polished, and iodized, by immersion in a solution of iodide of potassium, to which a little free iodine is added, will give very brilliant colors, by an exposure of several days. The process is quickened by mingling muriatic acid with the iodide. The results are singularly beautiful, the tone being of a furzy, velvety aspect. My best result was on a razor blade, which I attributed to the high polish. I hope for time to follow out this process. These pictures are greatly improved by exposure to the vapor of zinc.

EXPERIMENT 6.—*Nickel, Bismuth, and Antimony.* On each of these metals I obtained colors—but from the difficulty of procuring good surfaces of these metals, my experiments were limited. The method I employed was coating the metals with sulphuretted hydrogen, and then with bromine.

EXPERIMENT 7.—*German Silver, Prince's Metal, and Britannia.* Surfaces of these metals, in their purity, gave but indifferent results; but by alloying them with mercury—then with a solution of chloride of platinum—then with a weak solution of cyanide of silver—a compound was induced which gave some very startling results. With some plates thus prepared I obtained very brilliant colors instantaneously—but I found it exceedingly difficult to prepare the surfaces uniformly.

EXPERIMENT 8.—*The Alloy Plate.* The last experiment led me to devise an alloy plate, as follows;—I take a common daguerreotype plate, and polish the copper side of it. This side

I give an exceedingly light coating of silver, by means of the electrotype—just enough to give it a whitish blush. I then pour on it a very weak solution of nitrate of mercury, and let it rest a minute or two. Next I rinse the plate in water, and immerse it in a solution of cyanide of gold, made by dissolving 100 grains chloride of gold in 1 pint of water, in which has been previously dissolved 1 oz. cyanide of potash. I next expose the plate for some hours in a jar of chlorine gas, with a view of completely penetrating the superposed metals. Then I give the plate another light coat of silver in the same way as at first, after which I polish with a buckskin buff, and proceed to coat it with the vapor of iodine to a cherry red, and then over a jar of chloride of bromine to a bright green. This coating, I finish over the vapor of nitric oxyde, by keeping the plate over the gas from 5 to 10 seconds. A singular picture is produced by these means.

Experiment 9.—A plate prepared as in Ex. 8, will give a latent image, which is sometimes developed with very fine colors by exposure over the vapor of arsenic. This vapor may be generated by heating white arsenic in a tube of Bohemian glass. The tube must be short—not over three inches long. The vapor may be conducted into a shallow jar, and the plate placed on the open top of the jar.

Experiment 10.—*Iridium.* This singular metal forms an alloy with copper and gold. In this state I used a plate of it, as follows; I first rubbed it with a very little amalgam of silver and mercury. Then I coated it with chlorine gas to a dark green. This plate I exposed a few seconds to a colored image, and no apparent change appeared; but on a subsequent exposure over phosphuretted hydrogen, mixed with an atmosphere of vaporized sulphur, I obtained colors in great variety, but could never get a well defined and strong impression. The experiment is worth repeating—only, however, as a matter of scientific interest, as the rarity of the metal—Iridium—would prevent an extensive practical application of the process.

CHAPTER IX.

EXPERIMENTS WITH THE SALTS OF THE METALS.

Nitrate of Silver.—Great variety of processes by its means.—White Chloride of Silver.—Colored by the red ray.—Violet Chloride of Silver.—Its remarkable properties.—Chloro-Chromate of Silver—for Heliochromes on Paper.—How developed.—Colors strengthened by Hyposulphite of Gold.—Chromate of Copper—for Heliochromes in Red, Orange, Yellow, and Green.—Singular mode of developement.—Per-Manganate of Potash.—A "Chameleon" under Colored Light.—Chloride of Barium—its extraordinary Colorific effects.—Process with Silica.—Fluoride of Calcium and Precipitated Silver.

SECTION 1.—Among the "salts of the metals," nitrate of silver stands at the head of the list, for its utility as the foundation of a great number of processes. In forming other compounds of the metal, by mutual decomposition; in producing oxydized and silver surfaces, by reduction; and as a direct wash for paper, and other substances, as well as for its usefulness when in a state of excess, there is no question of its indispensable character. The particular facts which established this view of the great importance of this salt are abundant in the course of this volume.

SECTION 2.—*Chloride of Silver.* There are several varieties of this salt. I will first notice the white chloride, formed by mixing a solution of nitrate of silver and a chloride, as common salt, which is a chloride of soda. On exposing this to the colored rays, we are at once struck with the invariable fact that the red ray tints it its own color. The fact was known long time ago—but of this I was not aware when it turned up in the course of my experiments. Any person can test this fact in a very simple way. Soak for two or three minutes, a piece of paper in a solution of chloride of soda 10 grs. to 1 oz. water, and dry. Then float it for five or ten minutes on a solution of nitrate of silver, 50 or 60 grs. to 2 oz. water. Cover a portion of this with a red glass—or a piece of white glass, covered with some transparent red fluid, as carmine dissolved in ammonia; and leave the other portions exposed to the action of the white light for several hours. The latter portion of the paper will be blackened, while the former portion of it will be reddened. It cannot be doubted that this is a very remarkable fact, and is the natural color, if not the natural colors.

Ho n Silver is another variety of the chloride. It is made by simply melting the chloride. In this state it may be formed into a beautiful tablet, by pouring a layer of it on a polished surface, as glass. This tablet, exposed to the colored spectrum, is reddened much more strongly than the white chloride. Besides, it is tinted blue by the blue ray, and sometimes yellow and green, by yellow and green light.

The Violet Chloride of Silver is a still more remarkable substance. This may be produced by immersing a silver plate in a chloride, as that of copper, iron, or nickel, to the solution of which has been added some hydrochloric acid. Or, the white chloride may be converted into this by immersing it in the above acid, warmed slightly, for several hours. This violet chloride of silver, properly managed, will give all the colors of the spectrum. I discovered this fact long before M. Niepce de Saint Victor announced his discovery. The way I arrived at the discovery was as follows: For the purpose of experiment merely, I covered a daguerreotype with a solution of chloride of copper, and applied heat. The result was a beautiful ruby red coating over the daguerreotype, but so transparent that it did not dim the picture to any great extent. This picture was afterwards exposed in a window, and turned white. I took the hint—that is, I noted that the surface was photogenic, but I did not dream of its being heliochromic. I superposed upon another plate, prepared in the same way, an engraving (and it happened to be a colored one), and having exposed the arrangement to light I obtained a colored picture. The best way to conduct this experiment is to coat a plate as for taking a daguerreotype. Expose in a camera pointed to a white sheet, as long as you would to obtain a daguerreotype, mercurialize, and gild as usual. Then immerse the plate in the chloride, until it turns a dark maroon color, rinse in plenty of water, and heat the plate until the coating assumes a bright ruby red. Several of the daguerreotypes originally treated as above are still in my possession. The colors thus obtained are much better than those obtained by the afterwards discovered method of St. Victor. A thorough investigation of this matter would satisfy any reasonable person of my claim to priority in this matter of chloridizing a silver plate. St. Victor's originality, as far as I am concerned, I freely concede, but I totally deny his priority. To show the sincerity of this assertion, I have made oath to it, as the subjoined will indicate.

STATE OF NEW YORK,
Town of Lexington, } ss.
Greene County,

Before me, one of the Justices of the Peace of the County of Greene, personally appeared Levi L. Hill, and being duly sworn, says that he made the above discovery of a method of chloridizing a silver plate several months previous to the publication of M. Niepce de St. Victor's process of chloridizing a silver plate.

LEVI L. HILL.

Sworn to this 6th day of May, 1856,

ADAM MONTROSS, *Justice of the Peace.*

SECTION 3.—*Chloro-Chromate of Silver.* Dissolve 20 grs. common salt and 30 grs. of bi-chromate of potash in 1 oz. of water. Wash one side of paper with this solution, and let it dry. Then float one side of the sheet for a few seconds on a bath of nitrate of silver of the strength of three grains to the ounce of water. Float for a few seconds only, and dry in a dark room. Now repeat the washing with the saline solution, omitting the bi-chromate of potash. Dry, and float on a bath of nitrate of silver, 60 grs. to the oz. of water, for five minutes. Dry. All these operations, excepting the first washing, must be done by the light of a distant candle. After exposure to a colored image, for a few seconds, apply, by the light of a candle, a wash made as follows :—

1 oz. walnut shucks, dried and pulverized, and macerated 48 hours in 8 oz. water.

Add to this

2 grs. pyro-gallic acid,
$\frac{1}{2}$ oz. acetic acid—crystallizable,
4 drops oil of cloves, and 4 drops oil of cassia, dissolved in $\frac{1}{2}$ oz. alcohol.

After the picture is developed, it should be washed in water, and then soaked in the following bath until a decided strengthening of the colors results :

Sel d'or, 20 grs.
Water, 1 pint.
Muriatic acid, 1 drachm.

To fix these pictures a brief immersion in very weak ammonia, and subsequent washing in water, is all that is necessary.

SECTION 4.—*Chromate of Copper.* Dissolve 1 drachm sulphate of copper in 1 oz. of water. Add to this half an oz. of a saturated solution of bi-chromate of potash. Float one side of paper on this solution, and dry in the dark. Expose to a colored image until a strong negative picture is formed. Then the parts in red are to be touched with a camel's hair brush wet with a strong solution of nitrate of silver—say 100 grains to the oz. of water. The parts in orange and yellow are to be touched with weaker solutions of the nitrate. The greens are brought out by several washes of the part with warm ammonia. With a little practice and dexterity very fine results may be obtained by this process. To fix these pictures, soaking in water is sufficient.

SECTION 5.—*Permanganate of Potash.* Dissolve 100 grs. of this curious salt in 4 oz. water. Apply a wash of it to paper previously dipped in a strong solution of fish glue and dried. Dry rapidly, by holding it before a fire. Then wash the paper with a solution of 10 grs. nitrate of silver in 1 oz. water, to which has been added 1 drop of liquid ammonia, and 2 drops strong solution of bitumen of Judea in oil of lavender. This last wash should be applied, and the paper dried in a candle-lighted room. The paper in this state will remain good a long time if kept in darkness. When required for use apply a second wash of the above described silver solution, dry, and expose to a colored image until the picture is formed. In this process the glue, singular as the fact may appear, plays an important part, for, on ordinary paper, the same chemicals will not give coloration. The compound of the alkaline silver solution, the bitumen, the essential oil, and the glue, is somehow productive of a molecular arrangement favorable to coloration; and the manganese salt used (sometimes called "chameleon mineral," owing to the variety of colors afforded by its solutions), is in some way I cannot explain essential to the effect.

SECTION 6.—*Chloride of Barium.* This is another of those metallic salts which have peculiar colorific properties. It has long been noticed that the tone of common photographs is singularly enriched by salting the paper with chloride of barium. The following process has given me some beautiful results. I float paper a few minutes on a solution of chloride of barium—40 grs. to 1 oz. of water and 1 oz. of strong solution of gelatin. I then dry the paper until the gelatin surface becomes tacky, or until dry, and float it five or six minutes on a solution of nitrate of silver—100 grains to 1 oz. water. This paper is quite sensitive if used wet, and will give red, blue, and sometimes yellow and green. It requires a long time in the camera. For this purpose it may be kept wet by placing it between two plates of glass. Another way to obtain coloration on this paper, is to blacken the whole sheet in sun-light, bleach out the blackening in a solution of chloride of copper (observing to do the latter in a shaded room), and exposing to a colored image while the paper is still wet. Or if this paper is dried and then wet with essence of cloves, it will work very quick and give better results.

SECTION 7.—*Silica, Fluoride of Calcium, and Precipitated Silver.* If these are mixed in about equal bulks, and about one-half their whole weight of sulphuric acid added, there results a combination of singular colorific properties. The mixture should be intimately blended with wheat flour paste, and spread on paper or glass. After a protracted exposure to a colored image, a picture tinted in natural colors is produced. But if the latent colored image, formed by a much shorter exposure, is developed, by immersion in a very dilute solution of ammonio-chloride of copper, a much better picture results.

CHAPTER X.

EXPERIMENTS WITH VEGETABLE JUICES.

Red rose, violet, marigold, dandelion, dahlia, poppy, and peony, their coloring matter imparted to paper, sensitive to their colored rays.—Otto of rose an accelerator.—Instantaneous colored impressions on collodion, impregnated with the spirituous extract of the coloring matter of red poppy, clover blows, horse-chestnut leaves, etc.—Means of acceleration by sulphuretted air.—The heliochromy of the autumnal tints imitated.—Xanthophyl.—The coloring matter of leaves acted upon simultaneously by a freezing mixture and light.—The coloring matters of the blood beet, carrot, and red cabbage, give pictures in red, blue, yellow, and green.—Interesting results with the red tomato, strawberries, and collodion —Red top grass.—Potato starch and poke berries.—Bitter-sweet, blackberries, squawberries, and muriate of tin.—Alum as a mordant for vegetable colors.

Section 1.—Take a small handful of the leaves of the red rose, violet, marigold, dandelion, dahlia, poppy, and peony, and mash them in an earthen mortar with about half a pint of alcohol. Do this by the light of a candle only. Strain off the colored liquid, and keep it well corked in a glass bottle, in a dark and cool place. In this way it may be kept good for months. To use it, spread one side of paper with it, let the paper dry, and then spread it with alcoholic tincture of otto of rose—say one drop of the pure otto to half an ounce of alcohol. Let the paper dry spontaneously, and it is ready for use. It requires a prolonged exposure to the colored rays, but the resulting pictures are strikingly delicate and beautiful.

Section 2.—Take equal parts of red poppy, clover blows, horse-chestnut leaves, or the flowers named in the preceding section, and make an alcoholic tincture of their coloring matter, as directed above. Add a few drops of this to plain collodion, coat a glass in the usual way, instantly expose to a colored image for a second or two, and develope by immersing the glass in an alcoholic tincture of gallic acid, to which enough ammonia has been added to slightly redden the solution. This process is uncertain, but it is well worth further experiment.

Both of the above processes are quickened, by the addition to the first wash of a little otto of rose, or by sulphuretting the air of the camera box by means of a few drops of sulphurous acid, or, what is equally good, sulphuretted hydrogen. A small vial of hydrosulphuret of ammonia, left open in the camera box, answers very well.

SECTION 3.—The heliochromy of the autumnal tints may be imitated by impregnating paper with the expressed juice of leaves, grasses, &c. (See Xanthophyl.). The best way is to expose the wet paper to light and a powerful freezing mixture, simultaneously, a mixture of salt and ice answers well. The paper may be laid between two plates of glass, and the freezing mixture held against the back glass, while the front glass is exposed to a colored image. Or, the back glass may be subjected to a continuous stream of sulphuric ether, which will cause the chlorophyl to freeze. If the process is conducted expertly, and the two actions are simultaneous, you will frequently succeed in producing remarkable evidence of colorific action.

SECTION 4.—A mixture of the coloring matter of blood beet, carrot, and red cabbage, imparted to paper, gives pictures in red, blue, yellow, and green; but the process is slow, and the results not very good.

SECTION 5.—The juice of red tomato, or that of strawberries, gives remarkable results when mixed in suitable proportions with plain collodion, slightly tinctured with iodide of silver. The coloring matter should be extracted by alcohol, without much bruising of the fruit, as, in the latter case, you get so much water as to spoil the collodion.

SECTION 6.—Red Top Grass. The alcoholic tincture of the

red tops of this grass, imparted to paper, will give good red and blue, and sometimes all the colors. So, also, a mixture of freshly prepared potato starch and pokeberry juice, will sometimes give good results; but both processes are very slow, and I could never quicken them.

SECTION 7.—Bittersweet, blackberries, and squawberries, form a remarkable compound. Equal parts of their juices mixed, and imparted to paper previously soaked in dilute muriate of tin, have given me very brilliant colors.

SECTION 8.—I have found, in all these processes, great improvement by a first soaking of the paper in weak alum water. It seems almost to act as a mordant.

CHAPTER XI.

NATURAL COLORS ON PAPER.

Several methods of Silvering Paper.—Hydrogen Gas and Chloridated Paper. —Chromate of Copper Paper: how developed.—Interesting process with Chameleon Mineral, Chromate of Potash, Alum, and Nitrate of Silver.—Litmus Paper rendered Heliochromic.—Paper Heliochromes intensified.

1. *Silvering Paper.*—Soak paper in a solution of nitrate of silver, of the strength of 100 grains to 1 oz. of water. While moist, expose it in a jar of hydrogen gas or of phosphuretted ether, until the silver is reduced. If well done the paper will have a soft, silvery aspect, universally spread over its surface. A second soaking and exposure to the gas may be necessary. Another method is to soak paper in the above solution of nitrate of silver, and expose it while wet to direct sunshine, until the reducing process is effected. Or you may soak paper in iodide of potassa, five or ten grains to the ounce of water, dry, and soak in, or wash with the solution of nitrate of silver. Expose this for a second to diffuse light, and reduce the surface to the metallic state by soaking in a solution of proto-sulphate of iron, twenty grains to one ounce of water. In all the above processes the effect is better if the paper is previously glazed with a strong solution of fish glue. And strange as it may seem, the glue has a powerful influence upon the subsequent coloration.

2. Papers prepared as above, may be submitted wet to chlorine gas, in the jar containing a few drops of hydrofluoric acid. Or it may be soaked in a well filtered solution of chloride of lime, to which some solution of blue vitriol and a little muriatic acid

has been added. The soaking should be very brief, and the paper rinsed in abundance of water, and dried.

3. *Hydrogen Gas and Chloridated Paper.*—If after a sheet of paper is impregnated with chloride of silver, by washing with solution of common salt or other chloride, and then after drying with nitrate of silver, it is exposed to hydrogen gas, it acquires the property of being tinted by the colored rays. It is very curious that this effect is greatly heightened and accelerated by placing over the jar of hydrogen a deep red glass, and exposing the arrangement to sunlight. A good method is to wet the paper, and lay it on the under side of the glass. In this way red sunlight will strike every part of the paper.

4. *Chromate of Copper Paper.*—Mix 1 oz. of a saturated solution of bi-chromate of potash with 2 drs. of sulphate of copper, dissolved in 1 oz. of water. After shaking, filter the solution, and wash paper with the same. Dry and expose to a colored image, until a negative image appears, and develope by means of washing different parts with solutions of nitrate of silver of different strengths. In this way you will produce a great range of colors, from light yellow to a deep red. This process is decidedly pretty, and really beautiful pictures may be obtained by taking some pains.

5. *The " Chameleon process."*—Soak paper in a weak solution of " Chameleon mineral," dry ; soak in a half saturated solution of bi-chromate of potash; dry; soak in a strong solution of alum ; dry ; soak in a solution of nitrate of silver—one grain to an ounce of water—and dry. This paper, if the proportions are proper, affords interesting effects. The process is very slow.

5. The common blue litmus paper gives evidence of colorific properties, after treatment, first, with muriatic acid, and then with nitrate of silver. After the picture is formed, a characteristic effect is produced by touching parts of the image with a solution of carbonate of soda. The effect may be varied by

using a variety of alkalies, as potash, hyposulphite of soda, ammonia, &c.

I have invariably found that these pictures may be greatly intensified by immersion in a bath of sel d'or (hyposulphite of gold), after which, long soaking in water fixes the images.

CHAPTER XII.

HELIOCHROMES ON TEXTILE FABRICS.

Beautiful process on Cotton Cloth, Linen, or Silk, applied to the manufacture of Window Shades, and other Transparencies, in Colors.—Silk prepared with Nitrate of Silver and Per-muriate of Tin, and the picture developed with a compound of Chromic Acid.

1. Nothing can exceed in beauty some results I have obtained on cotton cloth, linen, silk, velvet, wood, and ivory. I proceed substantially as follows, viz:—I first imbue the substance with hot fish glue, and dry. Then I immerse it in a solution of sal ammoniac—ten grains to one ounce of water, and dry. It is then ready for the nitrate of silver bath, which should be of the strength of 100 grs. to 1 oz. of water. It is better to soak the article in this solution gently warmed. While wet, expose for one or two seconds to diffuse light, and then immerse in a solution of proto-sulphate of iron, 40 grs. to 1 oz. of water. Rinse in water, and soak for a few minutes in a solution of cyanide of potash—5 grs. to 1 oz. of water. Rinse, dry, and immerse for a few seconds only, in a solution of 1 oz. of sulphate of copper, and dry. Then immerse in muriatic acid, diluted with five parts of water, rinse, dry, and heat the article until it takes on a reddish brown hue. It is then ready to receive a superposed colored picture, which must be pressed closely upon it by a plate of glass, and exposed to direct sunshine for a period ranging from five minutes to half an hour. Soaking in water, to which a very little ammonia is added, is all that is necessary to fix the pictures.

2. White silk, sensitized with muriate of tin and nitrate of

silver, is susceptible of lively coloration, by a much shorter exposure to light.

3. The chromate of copper process described in the preceding chapter, may be turned to good account in its application to window shades, and other transparencies. After the picture is finished, the cloth may be rendered transparent by saturating it with a solution of equal parts of gum arabic, gum tragacanth, and white sugar.

The chromate of copper preparation described in the preceding chapter, is beautifully applicable to the same purpose.

CHAPTER XIII.

NATURAL COLORS ON GLASS.

Albuminate of Silver.—Blue Collodion —The Chromates and Collodion.—Beautiful Silvering of Collodion by precipitation of the metal.—Splendid Scarlet Red.—Coating of Collodion bleached by light, and giving colors in great strength and purity.—Method of developing these Pictures.

1. *Albuminate of Silver.*—Beat up to a froth the whites of 12 fresh hens' eggs mixed with one-fourth their bulk of water. Let this settle for 24 hours—decant the clear liquor—dissolve in it 60 grains chloride of baryta, and 20 grains of chloride of soda (common salt), and strain through fine muslin. Coat a clean glass with this mixture in the same way as you would with collodion. After it has drained a few minutes, heat the glass over a spirit lamp about as hot as you can bear your hand upon it. Let it cool, and immerse it in a bath of nitrate of silver, made in the following proportions :—

Nitrate of silver, 60 grains.
Water, 1 ounce.
Acetic acid, 1 drachm.
Hydrofluoric acid, 5 drops.

Keep the glass in this solution until the albumen appears a fine milk white. Expose this to diffuse light for about a minute—cover the plate with a solution made thus :—

Saturated solution of gallic acid, 1 oz.
Nitrate of silver solution, 10 grains to 1 oz. water, 20 or 30 drops.

This will produce an intense blackness over the entire coating.

Rinse the glass, soak a few minutes in a solution of hyposulphite of soda—1 oz. to 3 oz. of water—rinse, dry, and immerse the glass a few minutes in a bath made thus :—

Black oxyde of copper 1 oz.
Muriatic acid 4 ounces.
Dissolve the oxyde by the aid of heat.
Dilute the solution with 6 ounces of water, and filter.

After immersion in this bath, and rinsing, dry and heat the glass until it takes a pink hue.

This process gives very fine pictures; but it works slow, and I have not attained certainty with it.

2. *Blue Collodion.*—The ordinary collodion may be blued by impregnating it with chlorine gas. It should be done by injecting chlorine gas into a bottle of collodion. This collodion should be kept closely corked. A slight amount of bi-chromate of potash should be added to it—say half a grain of the salt dissolved in the least possible quantity of water—to every 5 ounces of the collodion. Coat a glass with this in the usual way, and immerse it in a bath of nitrate of silver, 50 grains to 1oz. of water. When the greasy look disappears from the glass, let it drain about one minute, and cover its surface with a solution of fish glue, and expose to a colored image.

3. *Silvered Collodion.*—Sensitize ordinary collodion, by adding to each ounce, 12 grains of iodide of potash, dissolved in the least possible quantity of water. Let it settle, after the addition of one drop of muriatic acid, and thorough shaking. Dip this in the above-described silver bath, for five minutes ; expose to light a few minutes, place it on a level support, and cover it with a solution of ammonio-nitrate of silver, made as follows :—

Nitrate of silver, 25 grs., dissolved in water, 1 oz.
Add ammonia, until a precipitate is formed and just re-dissolved, and then add 5 grains more of nitrate of silver to secure an excess.

To this mixture, add three drops oil of lavender, 2 drops oil of cassia, dissolved in 1 drachm of alcohol.

After covering the glass with this solution, drop upon it a few drops oil of cloves, dissolved in a little alcohol. Apply a gentle heat, and in a few minutes the collodion will be saturated with a coating of pure silver. Rinse and dry. Pour over it a solution of sulphate of copper, 40 grains to one oz. water, to which is added 50 drops of muriatic acid. Rinse and dry.

4. *Scarlet Collodion.*—Submit the plate just described to an oven heat of about 200° Fahr., until it acquires a brown hue. Then expose it under a ruby-red glass, to direct sunlight, until it has a scarlet color. It is then ready for the camera, or for a superposed colored picture. By a sufficiently long exposure, you will obtain a brilliant coloration, almost equal to what may be produced on plates.

By soaking the glass in weak ammonia, nearly saturated with iodide of silver, you may develope a picture after a very brief exposure.

I have worked the above process but little. It is new. But I have no doubt that this, or a modification of this process, will yet be the "*ne plus ultra*" of Heliochromy. It is yet a germ—but in skilful hands it will grow up a tree of mighty branches—a plant of renown and beauty, that will spread itself over the whole earth.

CHAPTER XIV.

THE HILLOTYPE.

As a Formula.—The Formula explained.—My method of working the Formula.

THIS name—"The Hillotype"—was first given to my process by S. D. Humphrey, Esq., editor of the Daguerrean Journal. He did so on his own responsibility. I called it, from the first, "The Heliochrome." Mr. Humphrey's godfather-ship has, however, been universally adopted by the public. I am now to detail the process known by Mr. Humphrey's cognomen, and will do so.

I.—AS A FORMULA.

1. Thoroughly clean a good daguerreotype plate, by means of rotten stone and alcohol. Polish with buckskin and calcined lampblack. Rouge is detrimental. For ordinary experimenting, you may omit the polishing.

2. Electrotype the plate till its surface assumes a deep blue. The ordinary cyanide of silver solution is far inferior to the following:—Mix solutions of the cyanides of silver, copper, and zinc, in the proportion of 8 parts of silver, 2 of copper, and 1 of zinc. Use two pair of Daniels batteries, and proceed in every other respect as for electrotyping an ordinary daguerreotype plate.

3. Rinse and dry the plate. If you use artificial heat to dry the plate, let the latter get cold before the next operation.

4. Place the plate on a level support, and cover it with a well filtered solution of nitrate of mercury—1 grain of the salt to 20

oz. of water. Let this remain on about half a minute. Pour it off and thoroughly rinse the plate, then cover it with a solution of sel d'or (hyposulphite of gold), 20 grains to one quart water, and let this remain on the plate about one minute. Rinse and dry, and again place the plate in the silver solution until it is slightly changed—say from one to five minutes—according to the strength of the solution. Rinse and dry, and buff to a polish, using calcined lampblack instead of rouge.

5. Now coat the plate over a jar of chloride of iodine—1 oz. chloride to 8 oz. water, until it assumes a bright pink color. Expose the plate a moment to diffuse light, or place it in a camera directed to a white screen as long as you would for a portrait, and then place the plate over mercury, heat to 170° Fah., for about three minutes. Wash with hyposulphite of soda—or, what is better, cyanide of potash, as you would for a Daguerreotype picture; rinse with water, and gild in the usual way with chloride of gold, or sel d'or. Rinse and dry. If you have exposed long enough to light, your plate will now have a bluish light cast, or solarization, similar to overdone linen in a Daguerreotype.

The whole of the above process will occupy but little more time than is required for producing and finishing an ordinary daguerreotype picture.

6. Expose the plate, prepared as above, in a jar of chlorine gas, until it takes on a faint yellow the second time. Keep the plate in this state in total darkness, until wanted for use. It greatly improves by keeping. The chlorine for the above coating I conveniently procure as follows, viz:—I wet several folds of cotton cloth with dilute sulphuric acid, and place them in the bottom of a deep jar. On these I spread one thickness of cotton flannel, dry, and over that I sprinkle about a teaspoonful of dry chloride of lime, and immediately close the jar. In a few minutes a sufficiency of chlorine gas will be evolved to coat the plate. The action will be mild and uniform.

7. Prepare the following "singular compound:"—In a quart bottle place 4 oz. of common salt, 4 oz. of blue vitriol, each well

pulverized, and add 16 oz. of water heated to 122° to 140° Fah. Shake well for five minutes, with the bottle well stopped. Set it aside to cool. When perfectly cold there should be a deposit of sulphate of soda. If there is not, place the mixture in an evaporating dish, and by means of a water bath, slowly evaporate, until, on cooling, a deposit of sulphate of soda takes place. Then decant the clear liquid into a clean bottle with a wide mouth. Fit into the mouth of the bottle the beak of a lead retort. In the retort place 2 oz. of fluoride of calcium, and 4 oz. of sulphuric acid, and apply a very gentle heat. The beak of the lead retort must dip into the liquid in the bottle, and the stem passed tightly through a well fitted cork. In a few minutes the liquid in the bottle will become saturated with fluo-hydric acid. The fumes of this acid are intensely poisonous, and the operation should be conducted with extreme caution. When the operation is over, let the retort cool, and immediately wash it with abundance of water. To preserve the liquid, it should be transferred to a gutta percha bottle. After the transfer, add to the liquid 4 oz. of pure muriatic acid, and ½ oz. black oxyde of copper. Cork tight, and let it stand at least 48 hours, with occasional shaking. Now mix, in an evaporating dish, 1 oz. of peroxyde of iron, (common rouge), 5 oz. of pure muriatic acid, and ½ oz. of yellow ochre, and apply heat until a deep yellow liquid is formed. Filter into a glass bottle, and add ¼ oz. of boracic acid, 60 grains of phosphate of soda, 30 grains of per-manganate of potash, ½ oz. of the fuming liquid of Libavius (made by saturating nitro-muriatic acid with tin by the aid of heat), 5 drops of pure bromine, and 3 grains of iodine. Agitate the mixture for about ten minutes, and add it to the other bottle. Shake well and filter. Place the clear liquid in a large earthen glass, or gutta percha platter, and keep it in sunlight until the watery portion is evaporated. The bottom of the dish will be covered with clusters of brilliant, green, needleform crystals. Collect, and keep these in a well stopped bottle. When you wish to form a bath for coating plates, dissolve 2 oz. of these crystals in 4 oz. of water, and add 1 oz. of pure muriatic acid, 1 grain of bi-chromate of potash, 3 grains of sel d'or, and ½ oz. of hydrofluoric acid. Shake well, and filter. Place this in an earthen glass, or gutta percha platter—tilt the platter so as to gather the liquid in one end of the dish—lay the plate prepared as in sec. 6, on the bottom of the platter, and lower the latter in such a way as to secure an even flow of the chemical over the plate. Suffer the plate to remain from 3 to 10 minutes, or until it appears nearly black. This should be done by the light of a candle only. Now rinse the plate freely with water, and dry it off with a spirit lamp, as you would finish a daguerreotype. In this state the plate will reproduce the colors, by a prolonged exposure to light, as you will see by pressing upon it a colored engraving by means of a plate of glass, and placing it in sunlight. Many of my experiments were performed in this stage of the process.

8. To render a plate, prepared as above, exquisitely sensitive, you have only to immerse it a few seconds in the following preparation, rinse, and dry. In 1 oz. of aqua ammonia dissolve 6 grains of gallic acid, add to this 1 drachm hydrosulphuret of ammonia, ½ oz. common salt, 1 drachm each of strong essence of lavender, cassia, and cloves, 2 drachms of grape sugar, 50 grains of fluoride of potash, 10 grains hyposulphite of copper, and a quart of water. This preparation may be used in a platter like the preceding. When not in use, it should be kept well corked. Its use gave me a great step in advance. It not only quickens the process, but adds greatly to the strength and truthfulness of the coloration.

9. A further great improvement in the strength and brilliancy of the pictures results from modifying the coating of the plate, as above prepared, by the application of heat, or by the action of the orange rays of light, or by both combined. If the plate is heated until it assumes a red, it gives the colors more brilliantly, and the whites are always good. A plate which would not give yellow and green, will give both after being exposed under a deep orange glass, in the sun, for a few seconds.

10. In forming a colored image on these plates direct, without a developer, a prolonged exposure is required—from five minutes to half an hour, in sunlight. Your true way will be to use the process thus, by means of superposing colored engravings, or other transparent objects, until you have thoroughly tested your chemicals, and mastered the process of coating. Then you may proceed to the work of developing the latent colored images, which you will soon be convinced, are formed almost instantaneously. Phosphuretted and sulphuretted hydrogen, and especially a mixture of carburetted hydrogen, phosphuretted ether, and ammoniacal gas, have the property of developing these images. So, also, with hot aqua ammonia, nearly saturated with hyposulphite of silver, and the combined vapors of burning copper, zinc, lead, and antimony. I make an alloy of these metals, and vaporize this alloy in a mercury bath, heat over a small charcoal furnace having a blast. The plate should be raised about 18 inches from the bottom of the bath. My apparatus for heating is an upright furnace, 10 inches in diameter. Attached to one side is a two foot balance wheel over which passes a band which turns a small shaft, and gives a rapid motion to a fan wheel 8 inches in diameter. The wheel is in a hollow disc having an opening in its sides to let in air. This disc discharges the blast through a tube entering the furnace. A common bellows, of good size, will answer.

The ammonio-hyposulphite of silver, named above, I use in a platter, placed over heat. It must be used at the temperature of 150° to 160° Fahr. The plate should be immersed in the liquid for a few minutes only. In this way I have produced some very fine results.

I use the mixed gases, above named, as follows. In a deep jar I place a few sticks of phosphorus, and cover them with sulphuric ether. The fume arising from it is phosphuretted ether. In the same jar I place a small bottle of aqua ammonia, and into the lower part of the jar I inject a small stream of carburetted hydrogen, made by mixing in a retort 4 parts of oil of vitriol with one part of alcohol, and applying a gentle heat. The plate should be held over this mixture for a period ranging from five minutes to half an hour. You may observe the progress by the light of a candle, screened by yellow glass or paper.

Phosphuretted and sulphuretted hydrogen (for the process of making which see chapter on chemicals), I employ in a similar manner, only the exposure need not be so long.

11. The final fixing and finish is given to these pictures as follows:

Dissolve in 1 quart water,
30 grs. hyposulphite of gold,
15 grs. chloride of zinc,
20 grs. sulphate of soda,
1 oz. sulphuric acid—pure.

Immerse the picture for a few minutes, or until a slight change is apparent. Then rinse the picture, dry, and rub it with a buckskin buff. A little sweet oil will heighten the polish. If you wish a dead surface, you have only to observe extreme cleanliness in the whole process, and omit the final polish.

II.—THE FORMULA EXPLAINED.

1. The first preparation of the plate has for its object the production of a peculiar molecular arrangement in the particles composing the surface. On this one thing—molecular arrangement—the whole phenomenon of coloration depends. Those who work the process, are urged to keep in view the fact that this preliminary method greatly conduces to the final grand result.

2. The "Singular Compound," described above I will not attempt to explain chemically. I will simply urge the absolute necessity of a strict adherence to the formula, both as regards manipulating, and the character of the chemicals. Lengthy as the process may seem, it is very simple.

3. The action of heat and of red light, in modifying the surface, is, I think, to disintegrate the coating, and to give it a different molecular structure. The result is an increase of sensitiveness; and this alone would seem to account for the superiority of the results, as to strength and brilliancy, and for the more certain re-production of yellow and green.

4. The quickening agents I have named may be greatly varied. The object of their use is to aid in reducing the silver compound formed to that condition at which colors are formed. It is difficult to tell what the compound on the plate is, but it is a peculiar compound of silver. Anything that will tend to reduce this salt to the state, or to the point where color forms, will quicken the process. Aldehide is one of the substances which deserve a thorough trial.

5. The action of the developers may be explained in a similar manner. I do not suppose that they produce color, but that they continue the molecular transformation of the surface commenced by the colored rays.

6. The fixing agent acts by way of deoxydizing the chemical surface. It also effects a partial decomposition of the surface, and those combined chemical agents, such as Chlorine, Fluorine, &c., which would otherwise re-act upon the picture, and destroy. All the pictures which I have treated thoroughly have remained fadeless. Those which have been carelessly done, have faded very much, and some of them have deteriorated in darkness.

III.—MY METHOD OF WORKING THE FORMULA.

1. In the choice of chemicals I am scrupulously nice. I set it down as a rule not to use a single chemical unless I am sure of its good quality.

2. I am very particular as to the clearness of bottles, dishes, &c., used in making and mixing chemicals. A little neglect here will defeat every other precaution. This is a hint of the utmost importance. It cannot be neglected with impunity.

3. I am equally particular in cleaning the plates. The polish is not of so much consequence; but an absolutely clean surface is indispensable. What I mean by a clean plate, is one free from such impurities as will injure the chemical effect. I have found no materials better than pure alcohol, good rotten stone, and clean cotton wool. If at any time you find a plate which has become stained in such a way, as that scouring will not clean it, heat it over a spirit lamp, until it whitens, and then scour it.

4. The chemicals I make in quantity—exactly in accordance with the formula, as I have given for them.

5. I avoid haphazard experiments. I make up my mind at night what experiment to try next day, and I stick to it till I have found the bottom of the idea, or till I am obliged to abandon it. No progress can be made in any other way.

6. I adopt, as a thing of no small importance, the principle—"creep before you walk." Hence I begin to work in the direct way—viz.—by superposing a colored print, and exposing until I get a picture without a developer. In this way I learn whether my chemical coating will give colors. This ascertained, I can pass to the developer, the quickening process, &c.

7. Perseverance, I have found, is a cardinal virtue in an experimenter. The moment we get discouraged, all progress is at an end. I have persevered for about nine years in the face of difficulties sufficient to appal stouter minds than mine, and all my success has depended upon my fixed purpose not to be foiled.

The foregoing statement of my formula, its explanation, and my method of working the formula, I have given in such a way as to avoid confusion, and at the same time to impart all necessary instruction. I have the fullest confidence in the success of all who bring to the process the aid of skill, industry, and perseverance.

CHAPTER XV.

MISCELLANY.

My Ambrotype Process—My Photographic Process—My Instantaneous Printing Process—My Transparency Process—My Toning Process.

The Ambrotype process here detailed is my own. I invented it in my own laboratory, before I heard of Mr. Cutting's success. It in no way interferes with his patent. Others have invented similar processes. Mr. Cutting doubtless invented his own. But to say that he has priority over his fellow artists, is nonsense. The more his claim is examined, the more absurd it appears. At least, I will guarantee my process not to infringe his alleged rights—and I will warrant it to work as good, if not better than his.

MY AMBROTYPE PROCESS.

Chemicals and Fixtures.—I purchase all my chemicals of Edwin Kent, 106 John Street, New York. Probably the stock dealers generally can supply the required materials. The importance of perfectly pure chemicals cannot be over-stated. One impure article will effectually prevent all success. The necessity of great cleanliness follows, of course. A slovenly manner of cleansing the bottles, dishes, etc., is equally fatal. The water used must be pure and soft. Good rain or spring water answers well.

Should any of my friends prefer to favor me with their orders, I will supply them on the following terms. The articles, including a complete outfit, in quantities sufficient for a good start in the business, will be sent by express to any part of the country, on the receipt of $15. All articles sent, warranted to be of the VERY BEST QUALITY. The following is a catalogue of said materials :

Prepared cotton—Daguerreotype cotton answers.
Sulphuric acid—Chemically true.
Nitrate potash—Refined.
Sulphuric ether—Concentrated.
Alcohol—95 per cent.
Iodide potash.
Bromide potash.
Nitrate silver.
Nitric acid.
Acetic acid.
Proto-sulphate of iron.
Cyanide potash.
Bi-chloride of mercury.
Chloride of ammonium.
Enamel—for backing.
Black varnish.
Nitrate of silver bath—Gutta percha.
Dipping rod— do. do.
Litmus paper.

The above articles are what I furnish. In addition you will require,

3 glass funnels.
1 porcelain mortar and pestle.
3 or 4 earthen platters—large enough for your largest size glass.
Half a dozen glass bottles—holding a quart each—with narrow mouths—and 2 or 3 with wide mouths.
1 graduated glass.

To make the Collodion.—Pulverize very fine, in your mortar, 3 oz. nitrate potash. To this add 2½ fluid oz. sulphuric acid. Stir it well, and after a minute or two, add 90 grains cotton. Mash this thoroughly for about 6 minutes. This should be done outdoors to avoid the fumes. Now take it out, with a strip of glass, and place it in a large earthen bowl of water. Stir it about, and keep changing the water, until a piece of litmus paper squeezed between the cotton is not reddened. Then place the cotton in the folds of a clean towel, and wring out the water. Next soak it in ether for a few minutes, and again wring. Repeat this two or three times with fresh ether. Cutting uses alcohol. Or, you may spread the cotton on clean paper, and dry it in the sun, or near (but not too near) a fire.

NOTE.—Wash the acid out of the cotton as quickly as possible; but be sure and get it all out, or you will fail in producing good effects.

To Dissolve the Gun Cotton.—Mix in a perfectly clean bottle (fluid measure,) 95 per cent. 6 oz. alcohol and 8 oz. sulphuric ether. Also 10 oz. of ether, and 5 oz. alcohol, forms a good mixture. Pull the cotton into shreds, add it to the mixture, and shake until solution takes place. This is collodion. Let it settle a day or two, and carefully decant for

Iodizing.—In a deep bottle, (clean and dry,) place 40 drops of pure soft water. Dissolve thoroughly in this, 20 grains bromide of potash. Then dissolve in this 20 grains iodide of potash. If the liquid turns milky, add water (by the single drop) until it is clear, and the iodide perfectly dissolved. Add 8 oz. collodion, and shake thoroughly. Let this settle about one day, and it is fit for use.

Or, mix 2 oz. ether and 2 oz. 95 per cent. alcohol—add to this equal weights of bromide of potash and iodide of potash, in quantity more than will dissolve. Shake a long time—say one hour—or until the liquid is saturated. Add the clear liquor to your collodion, until the glass will coat, by subsequent dipping in the silver bath, to a soft, creamy (not chalky) whiteness. This plan leaves your collodion clear, and ready for use. Perhaps, however, the first is the best plan for a beginner. The collodion, thus iodized, will turn red, from the effects of free iodine. To prevent this, or to restore it when reddened, keep a strip of sheet zinc, well cleansed, in the bottle—say half an inch wide and four or five inches long. In this way it will retain its working propensities for several months.

To quicken the collodion so that it will work instantaneous, add to each oz. of it, after iodizing, 1 drop of iodide of iron, prepared thus :—In a 4 oz. bottle place 2 drachms of iodine, 3 drachms iron filings, or some clean iron wire, and 2 oz. of a half and half mixture of alcohol and water. Shake frequently for a day or two, or until the liquid acquires a green tinge. If the iron should all dissolve, add more, so as to keep an excess of iron.

To Prepare the Silver Bath.—Measure off, in your graduated glass, the number of ounces of water necessary to fill your bath nearly full. Place this in a large bottle or pitcher, and dissolve in it pure nitrate of silver, in the proportion of 30 grains to 1 oz. water. Saturate this with iodide of silver, made thus :—Dissolve 30 grains nitrate of silver in one or two oz. water; dissolve 40 grains iodide of potash in the same quantity of water. Mix, and wash the precipitate in several waters. Decant the water, and add the precipitate to your silver solution. Agitate for an hour or two, filter (through clean paper, or cotton wool, previously wet, and pressed loosely into your funnel), and add to each 2 oz. of solution 1 drop of nitric acid. Your bath is now ready, and will work well, if you add, once in a week or two, a few drops of nitric acid. You can always test the acidity of your bath, by dipping into it a piece of litmus paper. It should produce a decided reddening of the paper.

Filter your bath every three or four days. Keep it out of the light, as much as convenient, and never suffer a dirty glass, or other impurity, to enter it.

The Developer.—Provide a clean pint bottle, with a wide mouth, and place in it 1½ oz. grains proto-sulphate of iron, pulverized, and 14 oz. water. Shake till the salt is dissolved. Then add 20 drops nitric acid, 1 oz. alcohol, and 3 oz. of acetic acid, and shake. Filter thoroughly through cotton or paper. When this works weak, add a few grains proto-sulphate of iron. An increase of the nitric acid gives more brilliant tones, but an excess of it produces fogging. The developer improves by use.

The Fixing Bath.—In one quart of water dissolve 1 oz. cyanide of potash. In this dissolve 10 grains nitrate of silver and 3 grains chloride of gold. Filter and keep in a platter (earthen or gutta percha) for use. It should fix the picture in 10 to 20 seconds. Occasionally add a small lump of cyanide of potash, but do not use the bath too strong. Or you may add strong hyposulphite of soda solution.

Taking the Pictures.—1. Cleanse and dry your glass thoroughly. Nitric acid and a little rotten stone make the best cleaning and scouring materials. Mix the two into a paste, and apply with a swab. Rinse with water, and dry with a clean towel, kept for the purpose. The best way is to clean and rinse a large number at once. Let them drain and dry, and when you wish to use a glass, rub it with a dry towel—frequently breathing on it, to assist in detaching any remaining scurf. Dust it with a large camel-hair brush.

2. Now seize the glass by one corner, between the thumb and finger of the left hand, and, holding it level, pour upon the centre a quantity of iodized collodion sufficient to spread over the whole surface. Tilt the glass so as to spread the collodion to each corner. Then pour the excess back into the bottle, from the corner opposite the thumb and finger. As the corner rests in the mouth of the bottle, give it a tilting motion, to prevent the collodion drying in lines. Hold the glass in the air for a minute or two, or until the collodion appears neither wet nor dry, when it will have some solidity, as you will perceive by pressing one corner of it with your finger. It is now ready for the silver bath.

3. Coating the glass may be done in the light, but in sensitizing in the silver bath all daylight should be excluded. Place the collodionized glass in your dipping rod, and immerse it with a steady plunge in the silver bath. Leave it there about a minute,

and examine it by the light of a candle or lamp. If it looks greasy, return it to the bath, and move it up and down until the greasy look is gone, and the coating assumes a bluish white, creamy appearance. Then, or not long after, place it in the plate frame, collodion side down, and cover the whole opening with a clean black cloth (to shut out light from the edges of the glass) and then button it down with the cap. It is now ready for the camera. Keep your plate frame, cap, and the cloth perfectly clean, otherwise it will soil the back of the glass, and soon spoil your developer.

NOTE.—Nothing is so good for the final cleaning of the glass as a solution of cyanide of potash—say 10 grains to 1 oz. of water. Rub it over the glass, and work it off with a clean towel, or good tissue paper.

Developing.—Hold the glass over a platter, and pour the developer on one corner, in such a manner as to flow over the surface at once; or immerse it in the developer, and keep the platter tilting, to prevent specks from settling. One or two minutes, and a much shorter time where the glass has a very full exposure, is a sufficient time to bring out the image in perfection. Sometimes the developing solution will get out of order, without any apparent cause. In this case you had better make a fresh supply. Always filter your developer for every glass.

Fixing Solution.—Lay the glass in this solution (which is best used in a platter), and let the liquid flow over it, back and forth, until the picture is cleared. The milky cloud which shows itself under the operation of the solution, is your guide. When this is all gone the operation is complete. Before immersing the glass in this bath, and after taking it from the developer, rinse it well with water. After fixing rinse again very thoroughly, and stand up to dry, or dry with a spirit lamp.

Backing.—Pour upon the collodion side of the picture a quantity of mastic or other quick drying varnish, in the same way you collodionize a glass. Let this dry, and repeat the operation with black Japan varnish. You can then place the glass in a case, and cover it with a mat.

Note.—Before applying the white varnish the glass should be well warmed. In place of the black varnish, you may hold the side having on the white varnish over burning turpentine. This will strike into the white varnish and form a beautiful black enamel. It has the advantage of never cracking.

MY PHOTOGRAPHIC PROCESS.

I. For taking superb Negatives you have only to vary the Ambrotype as follows:

1. Use a thicker collodion. This is secured by using less ether and alcohol in dissolving the gun cotton—say 6 oz. of ether and 4 oz. of alcohol.

3. Time longer—say twice or three times longer—than for Ambrotypes.

4. Leave on the developer much longer, as long as there is any increase of strength to the picture, and then much longer—say two or three minutes—that the picture may bear the action of the fixing agent.

II. For printing paper Positives, proceed as follows:

1. Select the best Photographic paper.

2. Pass it two or three times through the salting solution and hang it up to dry. No better salting solution can be made than 5 grains of common salt to 1 oz. of water. A quantity of this solution—say 1 or 2 quarts—may be placed in an earthen platter and the paper dipped a few times through it.

3. The silver solution is made thus: Dissolve 2 oz. nitrate of silver in 16 oz. water; place one ounce of the solution in a separate vessel; add aqua ammonia to the 15 oz. till a precipitate is formed and just re-dissolved, then add the other ounce of solution and shake; filter and place it in an earthen or guttapercha platter. Float the best side of a sheet of salted paper on this solution for five minutes and hang it up to dry. In placing the

sheet on the solution hold it by two opposite corners, lower the middle first and press down until the sheet lies flat; in this way you will avoid air-bubbles.

4. Place the sheet of paper after it is well dried, the silvered side up, on your printing frame,* lay your negative on it, collodion side down, and apply the springs to the side of the glass; then place the arrangement in the sun, or in a strong light, and examine it occasionally. When it is a little deeper than you desire it to finish, remove it and it is ready for

MY TONING PROCESS.

1. Soak the picture five minutes in water, then rinse in fresh water.

2. Place in a bath of 1 quart of water and 2 dms. aqua ammonia; watch it close, and as soon as it turns to a brick red tint, and before it is weakened, place it in fresh water for a minute.

3. Remove it to a bath of 1 quart of water, 1 bottle of sel d'or, and 2 dms. pure muriatic acid.

4. As soon as it acquires the desired tone place it in a solution of hyposulphite of soda, 8 oz. to 1 quart of water.

5. In five or ten minutes place it in water, and keep renewing the water for at least half an hour. Dry.

6. If you wish a glaze on the finished picture float it on a strong, clear solution of fish glue, and hang it up to dry.

MY INSTANTANEOUS PRINTING PROCESS.

Carefully prepare the following solutions, and label them Nos. 1, 2, 3, 4.

No. 1. Water 16 oz., iodide of potash 80 grains. Float the marked side of the sheet on this solution for two minutes. Dry.

No. 2. Water 16 oz., nitrate of silver 100 grains.

* Printing Frames can be bought of the stock dealers.

No. 3. Water 16 oz., gallic acid as much as the water will dissolve by long shaking. Mix a small quantity of these two together, and float the paper on it two or three minutes. Do this by the light of a distant candle, carefully excluding all other light. Dry. In this state the paper will keep in the dark for a long time. It will be of a light yellow color.

No. 4. Water 8 oz., nitrate of silver 300 grains, acetic acid half an ounce. Float the paper on this a few minutes—from 2 to 5; dry it off between several changes of blotting paper, or let it dry spontaneously. It is now ready for the printing frame.

Expose to light from one second to one minute, and proceed to develope by floating the paper on or washing with either No. 5 or No. 6.

No. 5. Saturated solution of gallic acid 1 oz., aceto-nitrate of silver (No. 4), 2 drachms. Mix, and use immediately.

No. 6. Water 16 oz., proto-sulphate of iron 300 grains, acetic acid 1 oz., alcohol 1 oz., nitric acid 50 drops.

As soon as the picture is sufficiently developed place it in water for a few minutes, and then in a solution of hyposulphite of soda —10 oz. of the salt to 20 oz. of water. Let it remain in this for 10 minutes or half an hour. Remove it to a dish of water, and change the water repeatedly for an hour. Dry and finish as usual.

MY TRANSPARENCY PROCESS.

These pictures are very beautiful and may be used for a variety of purposes. They are best seen by transparency, in other words by holding them up to the light and looking through them. With a black ground under the glass they show as negatives, but a white ground makes them positive.

These pictures are the best magic lantern sliders ever used. A landscape view, magnified by a lantern and thrown upon a screen, has all the appearance of nature. The pictures can be readily colored by the use of the transparent colors, and then they are an infinite advance on the old daubs commonly used for phantasmagoria.

The following is my method of producing these gems. Collodionize a glass as for a negative photograph—that is, proceed in every respect as directed under the Ambrotype process, only use thick collodion. On this glass procure a good negative of the object you wish in transparency—say a landscape or living person. Now prepare another glass in the same way. Have your negative placed upright in a strong light—say in a window so you can look through it. Place your quarter camera tube on your whole size box, and focus the negative on the ground glass the size you wish the picture, and insert your collodionized glass in the usual way. Expose a sufficient time to cause the picture to develope almost instantly.

The developer I use is prepared thus:

Water 1 oz.,
Pyro-gallic acid 2 or 3 grains,
Acetic acid 1 drachm.

Or you may use the proto-sulphate of iron as directed for Ambrotypes; but the pyro-gallic acid is much the best.

The fixing is done in the way directed for Ambrotypes. Then, after rinsing the picture, if you pour upon it a solution of sel d'or, 1 bottle to 25 oz. of water, and let this remain on a few minutes, you will find an astonishing improvement in the strength and tone of the picture.

This is the whole process. Nothing can be more simple, and as for the results they will speak for themselves.

I have referred to the use of these pictures for magic lantern sliders. Without any doubt a collection of views, portraits, insects, animals, birds, fish, microscopic objects, &c. &c., could be got together with but little expense, and form an exhibition of the most interesting character, which would be a fortune to any enterprising person who would go through the country with it.

I will name another application of the process. What could be more exquisitely beautiful than these pictures taken on large glass and used in windows, in place of the clumsily wrought devices we often see? They would sell extensively for this purpose.

CHAPTER XVI.

DESCRIPTION OF THE PHOTOGRAPHS.

The House—The Village—The Author.

1. *The House.*—What shall I say of the house? I have lived in it twenty-one years. "Of course," says the reader, "you must have liked it." That's true—and I do still, not because of its fine model, however; that, be it observed, is not exactly *au fait.* I will tell you how it came to be modelled after this fashion. The house originally consisted of a story and a half and a wing. The other main part was built in another part of the lot, and I occupied it as a printing office. Little did I then dream, as I pursued my daily toil at "type-sticking," that I would afterwards stick natural colors on silver plates in the same building. Well, having no more use for it as a printing office I "made a bee," and had it moved to where you now see it; the skylight I added afterwards. All told, this is a very convenient domicile. I shall soon leave it for another home; and I part with it as I would with an old friend. It has sheltered me and mine from many a summer solstice and many a wintry blast, and I love it for what it has done for me; and I, at least, admire this picture of it.

2. *The Village.*—The photograph presents a view of the village from the mouth of the remarkable mountain pass called the "big hollow." Those who have visited Westkill will at once recognise the view here presented. Westkill is truly "inclosed around about" by mountains; these mountains are branches of the

Catskill. Our village lies about 20 miles south-west of the "Mountain House." For true romantic beauty it cannot be surpassed. In the summer it is not only beautiful but remarkably healthy; in winter the climate is severe and changeable, and the whole aspect of the place is that of extreme dreariness. I can speak of the society as being, on the whole, remarkably good.

3. *The Portrait.*—The most I can say of this is that it is a pretty good fac-simile of the author's face. I cannot call it a very good-looking phiz; still, if you could add life to this photograph you would see it is not so bad.

THE END.

www.ingramcontent.com/pod-product-compliance
Lightning Source LLC
LaVergne TN
LVHW011227110826
845150LV00006B/1570

9781425514990